WANTING
MORE

WANTING MORE

The Challenge of Enjoyment in the Age of Addiction

MARK CHAMBERLAIN, Ph.D.

SHADOW
MOUNTAIN®

Visit us at www.shadowmountain.com

Library of Congress Cataloging-in-Publication Data

Chamberlain, Mark D.

    Wanting more: the challenge of enjoyment in the age of addiction / Mark D. Chamberlain.

      p.   cm.

    1. Quality of life. I. Title.

BF637.C5 C472 2000
155.4'2—dc21

                                     00-056341

Printed in the United States of America   18961-6706

10 9 8 7 6 5 4 3 2 1

To Helen Keller
You taught us to walk with more awareness
on the path we thought we knew

Contents

Introduction: A View from the Trailhead ix

Part I: How Enjoyment Eludes Us 1

  1 We Fail to Appreciate What We Have 3

  2 Our Enjoyment of Bodies and Beauty Gets Derailed 7

  3 We Can Never Get Enough 13

  4 Appetite's Seductive Lie 16

  5 The Intensity Trap 22

  6 The Age of Addiction 29

  7 When the Machinery Is Out of Order 37

Part II: Expanding Enjoyment 45

  8 Coming to Our Senses 47

  9 Reclaiming the Joy of Movement 55

  10 Enjoying What We Do 60

  11 Becoming Independent of Raw Material 64

  12 Recovering from Too Much 68

  13 Discovering Hunger's Hidden Treasures 72

  14 Standing Up to Desire 84

  15 Heeding the Voice of Conscience 92

  16 Protecting Enjoyment's Machinery 97

  17 Waking Up to the Abundance Right before Us 104

  18 Enjoyment's Paradoxical Pace 108

  19 Cultivating Awareness 113

  20 Sensitivity Breeds Delight 120

  21 Delighting In People 127

Epilogue: A Final Signpost 133

Sources Cited 135

Index 141

Introduction: A View from the Trailhead

What do you enjoy the most in life? What gives you that feeling of utter delight, the sense that you got everything just right—at least for the moment? What in your life has the power to keep you coming back again and again for more?

For me, buying a record album used to do it. I remember rubbing my hands across the shrink-wrap cover of a brand new Boomtown Rats album, then piercing the plastic with my thumbnail and immersing myself in the smell that comes with something so new. Complete satisfaction was mine before I even put the thing on the turntable.

Listening to some records for the first time was a disappointment: "So the song they play on the radio is the only good one of the bunch?" Usually, though, there were several songs that were a pleasure to hear. When that happened, I found it was possible to enjoy the album even more the second, third, and fourth time through. Each time I might hear something new—some off-rhythm thing the drummer was doing or the undercurrent of the bass guitar. For a time, repetition brought even more satisfaction.

Regardless of how ecstatic I was with an album at first, however, over time the pleasure inevitably faded. I remember picking up the stylus on the turntable and putting it back to the beginning of a favorite tune because I had just heard the entire thing without really enjoying it—or really even noticing that it was playing. Unfortunately, paying attention more closely couldn't bring back the initial feeling of excitement. It had escaped and would never return with the same intensity again. That record might sit on the top of my dresser for a while, being played less frequently all the time, until it finally made its way to the bottom of the stack on my bookshelf.

If we don't quickly distract ourselves with another purchase, launch into a new project, or strive toward a new plateau in some other way, we will notice a distinct sense of mourning in the wake of our most thrilling acquisitions and attainments. Our soul whispers—at times even cries out—"Is this all there is? *I want more!*"

When I was in my early twenties and thought about the prospect of marriage, I must admit I was more than a little concerned. I had seen enough divorces to know that people's feelings for their spouses could fade the same way my feelings about any given collection of songs had. And what about committing to a profession? How could I ever ensure that my sense of enthusiasm wouldn't lag in that area of life as well?

Have you also worried and wondered? Worse yet, have you discovered ugly truths that you never suspected? Has your perfect job turned dull and tedious? Is your dream home becoming just another place you have lived? Are you searching for the right lover—for the third time? Have you become disillusioned and concluded that enjoyment cannot live up to its promise? Have you come to believe that pleasure is unsustainable?

In my psychotherapy practice, I work every day with clients struggling with addictions and compulsive behaviors. Together we explore the way their satisfaction has faded even as they intensified their quest for it. Part one of this book is about this paradox: Increasing the intensity of stimulation in our lives can actually spoil our capacity for enjoyment.

Part two is about another paradox, a complement to the first: Tolerating less stimulation in our lives can actually increase our pleasure. I remember when this possibility first occurred to me. I was listening to a National Public Radio program about Helen Keller and was struck by how rich and full and thrilling she found life to be despite the lack of stimulation available to her. My addicted friends who wanted more found less, I marvelled, while Helen Keller found joy in a life seemingly more deprived than most of us can even imagine.

In the pages that follow, I hope to convince you that our enjoyment of life depends less on what we obtain or attain and much more on how we respond to that regularly recurring feeling that we don't yet have quite enough. We will be exploring how to enhance our enjoyment by accepting wanting as a part of life and not as a sign that we are not yet in the right place or in possession of the right stuff. We will also explore how to find greater pleasure and joy by cultivating our appreciation for the abundance all around us, the abundance we so often miss in this age of overstimulation, indulgence, and instant gratification.

Whether you are among those of us who have suspected that enjoyment might be out of our reach, or those of us just hoping to solidify our grip on it, you'll be happy to hear that our prospects are excellent. We need not worry that we are doomed to watch helplessly as our love for a spouse loses steam; we can do something to prevent it—in fact, we can do just about everything that needs to be done. We need not wonder whether our profession can possibly hold a career's worth of excitement; we can ensure that it does. The good news—*the great news*—is that we are not dependent for pleasure on the raw material in our lives. I pass this on as one who has tasted the good life: I now *know* whereof I speak. I have not yet enjoyed an entire lifetime, but I have seen enough to know that it can be done. Enjoyment, I have discovered, is up to us.

PART I

How Enjoyment Eludes Us

1

We Fail to Appreciate What We Have

In our modern society, despite the visible excesses and conspicuous consumption of so-called pleasure-seekers, we have not really learned to enjoy ourselves.
—Robert Ornstein and David Sobel

In your mind's eye, can you picture your dream home? Perhaps it has a spacious yard with lush vegetation. Maybe it's built of the finest materials and filled with beautiful decor and inspiring artwork. Don't forget the huge windows that provide a breathtaking view. Is that image somewhat different from the place where you live now? Who among us hasn't felt that we would be so much more content and fulfilled if we could just afford our dream house?

I'm thinking of one famous couple who were wealthy enough that they were able to turn their dream into reality. In the mid-1990s they purchased fifty-six acres in New York and built a home with two swimming pools, seven fireplaces, and nine bedrooms. Oh, and it had a recording studio as well. Starting to sound like something you've seen in your dreams? They must have lived in bliss for a while: They were both successful, in love, and living together in a virtual palace. But it didn't last. By 1998 they had divorced, moved out, and sold the home. Some months later, I read in the paper that the house had burned to the ground. Fortunately, it was vacant at the time, and there were no injuries. Yet the incident was still tragic: an empty, nine-bedroom mansion going up in flames—a tragic reminder that even our wildest dreams becoming reality may not be enough to satisfy us.

During my junior year in college, I worked for a real-estate appraiser. Part of my job was to drive around and take pictures of houses that had been sold recently. These photographs would be included in my boss's report on the house he was appraising, to show what houses of similar value in the area looked like. When I first started doing that work, it was quite a treat to see a $250,000 home. A quarter of a million dollars could build an impressive home; at least that was what I thought at first. It didn't take long, however, before I was no longer so easily impressed. Pretty soon, seeing those homes was just a mundane part of my job. But a $400,000 home could get my juices flowing. Now, *those* houses were nice. For a while. Until nothing under a half a million was very exciting anymore.

I talked with one of the appraisers at the firm about my changing taste in houses. "I'm getting harder and harder to please," I surmised, "harder and harder to impress."

"Actually, you're fortunate," he responded. "I have seen people waste a lot of money to learn the lesson you have learned without spending a dime." He told me about customers who buy their dream home, only to call him a few years later for an appraisal on a bigger and better house that they hope they will like even more. Those who can afford to continue to escalate in step with their appetite eventually discover that there is *always* a sense that even more would be better. Those who cannot afford to "upgrade," on the other hand, may never have the illusion challenged that the right house would be the key to their lasting happiness.

One day I was assigned to photograph three homes in the area that had each sold for over one million dollars. What a treat that was! Later that week my boss invited me to accompany him to complete the appraisal of one of those million-dollar houses. We photographed it from all angles and measured it inside and out. I will never forget that experience. In the yard there was a playground that was more elaborate than the one in the city park. The kids' bedrooms were filled with amazing toys. But I was puzzled. On the walls I saw pictures of a family of six, it was a beautiful summer morning and I knew school was out for the year, and yet there were no kids in sight. We finally found them when we were almost finished with our work. As we entered the spacious family room, I could see them huddled over in the corner. There all four of them sat, staring at the television set, with videocassettes strewn about them on the floor.

Thinking back on that scene now, I am reminded that in surveys, relatively affluent children generally give lower ratings of happiness than children at the lowest socioeconomic levels. Considering that experience also brings to mind the research conducted by Thomas Stanley and William Danko that they describe in their book *The Millionaire Next Door*. They discovered that the second-generation wealthy, as they age, often fail to enjoy their abundance. Instead, many of them live in fear of losing their wealth and are driven by an anxious desire to maintain the status quo rather than a soulful searching to cultivate and expand the good in their lives.

The truth is, we cannot simply enjoy life more by accruing more goods and goodies. Just as the float in a toilet tank rises with the water level to seal off incoming water and prevent overflow, our expectations seem to float upon our rising prosperity and shut down our pleasure with each step up we take. Illustrating the operation of this process are the findings from a 1990 Gallup poll that questioned respondents about how much money it took to make someone rich. On average, people estimated that 21 percent of Americans were rich; however, virtually none of the respondents placed *themselves* in that category. Less than 1/2 of 1 percent considered that they were rich, while the rest set the qualifying mark above their own income level. Along similar lines, in 1987 pollsters commissioned by the *Chicago Tribune* asked people what level of income would satisfy them. Would $50,000 a year do it? Most of those with current incomes of $30,000 thought that would be enough. So what about those who were already making $100,000? Wouldn't they be twice as happy with their pay as those with lower incomes were hoping to someday be? Hardly. They said they would need $250,000 to be satisfied ("Pay Nags," 10B; "Rich Think Big," 3).

The long-term satisfaction levels of former lottery winners provide perhaps the most compelling demonstration that pleasure and enjoyment can fade despite even dramatic jumps in prosperity. Many people are surprised to learn that those who have changed from average wage-earners to millionaires in a day don't rise to a new level of life enjoyment and then remain there perpetually. Instead, they are ecstatic initially, enjoy life more than usual for a few weeks, and then typically report a happiness level that has returned to whatever it was before their big win. An annoying and unfortunate side-effect accompanies their new enjoyment set-point, however: Lottery winners typically give lower enjoyment ratings than the rest of us do to the mundane, day-to-day activities of life.

Does it surprise you that the affluent don't necessarily find their lives more satisfying than their poorer counterparts? If you are like almost every one of us and have greater financial prosperity as one of your cherished goals, doesn't it trouble you that those who do obtain the most don't always enjoy it? Apparently it is very difficult to enjoy what we have once we have a lot. However, even if it is difficult, most of us would gladly accept the challenge. We'd like the opportunity to prove that we could handle wealth, that success wouldn't spoil us.

Well, guess what? We have the chance! The truth is, we are already wealthy. Even the poor among us have more than most other people on the planet, than most other people throughout history. There will always be those who have more than we do, always giving us the excuse to look up from what we have and stare wistfully at what they have. However, as we will explore further in the chapters to come, we will see that there is enough to appreciate right before us if we will simply take a few moments to consider our abundance.

Our Enjoyment of Bodies and Beauty Gets Derailed

Everything has its beauty, but not everyone sees it.
—Confucius

Haven't we all at some point identified a part of our bodies that we would change for the sake of appearance? Hasn't each one of us uttered at least one of the following critiques?

"I'm too fat."

"I'm not toned enough."

"My hair is too straight."

"I'm too skinny."

"My nose is too big."

"My hips are too wide."

"But," you might insist, "I only complain about my appearance because I *really am* too fat (thin, straight-haired, etc.)! If I could change my body in this way or that, I would be perfectly satisfied." If that is true, what level of attractiveness would we have to attain before we would be content? To find out, let us consider the folks whose appearance comes closest to the ideal and check out their level of satisfaction. Surely if we could have one of the most attractive bodies in the entire world, we would have nothing left to complain about, nothing left to desire, right?

Every year *People* magazine identifies the fifty most beautiful people in the world. Tom Cruise, Mel Gibson, and John F. Kennedy Jr. have been members of that elite group five times. But there is only one individual who made the list six times by the turn of the century. Perhaps as close as we mortals come to the mythological Helen of Troy, she is Michelle Pfeiffer, by all accounts a beautiful woman. Now, someone in her position must be satisfied, right? Yet she confided in an interview with the magazine when they picked her for the sixth time that she would change a thing or two about her body if she could. She would give herself longer legs. And "I really would like curls," she said (*"50 Most Beautiful"*).

Pfeiffer is not unique. I recently read an interview with Anita Ekberg, sex symbol of the 1960s, whose buxom figure was showcased in dozens of movies. Despite her success, she had her complaints. "I would like to have had a smaller bust. You dress better, you look better." Her body wasn't her only complaint. She would like to have won an Oscar. "How come they've given an Oscar for career to Sophia Loren? I've been in the movie business longer than Sophia, and nobody has thought to give me one" ("Anita Ekberg Looks Back," 14).

Faced with a sense of dissatisfaction and a desire for a better body, many people decide they don't have to put up with aspects of their physical appearance that they don't like. Unfortunately, working to alter our appearance often leaves us facing the same dilemma as the ambitious home buyer: As we progress, our goal seems to recede again with every step we take. And so a body builder's biceps may never be quite big enough, and he persists in feeling that twenty more minutes a week at the gym would do the trick. A young woman loses ten pounds on a diet only to conclude that another ten pounds would make her look even better. I'm sure no one ever walks into the hospital for his or her first cosmetic surgery thinking, "Why don't I plan to come back for about seven more of these after this one's over!" Yet, somehow, many do. Each one promises more gratifying results than the last, and the revolving door keeps turning.

This spiral can operate just as powerfully in the way we adorn our bodies. We can never have just the right number and variety of shirts or pairs of shoes in our closet—there's always one more shopping trip we just have to make.

When it comes to the way we look, better than before is never quite good enough. That is because the enjoyment we gain from appearance is, at best, fleeting. This is true not only of our own appearance but when we enjoy the appearance of others. We may seek out beauty for its thrilling effect, but with exposure and time it becomes less stimulating to us. When an individual views pornography, for example, he may initially be excited by the beauty of the bodies he sees. However, research has shown that individuals who are exposed to pornography over even a brief period come to rate their own mates as less attractive by the end of the study than they had at the outset. They even rated the amount of love they felt toward their mates as lower than they had before (Gutierres, Kenrick, and Goldberg, "Adverse Effect"). Overstimulation, although it brings immediate gratification, plants the seed for long-term dissatisfaction.

I gained some insight into our tendency to grow dissatisfied and bored with our beloved when I read some research on a chemical called phenylethylamine, or PEA. When we are infatuated, PEA is released into our body and brain, and it gives us a high as real as that from any drug. Our thinking can deteriorate under the influence of this chemical just as surely as it would if we were to drink alcohol or ingest some other intoxicating substance. We might make decisions that strike the "sober" people around us as impetuous. And yet we ourselves are convinced that we are on the right track, the correctness of our decision "verified" by the potent good feeling we are experiencing. Isn't this how affairs and divorces are so often justified?

However, our brain is never bathed in PEA for long. Like a time-release capsule with a divinely set deadline, the good feelings that accompany infatuation inevitably fade. People who buy into the illusion that they should always find their lover's appearance as appealing as they did at first are generally disappointed within a relatively brief time. This is why the most attractive people among us may be at somewhat of a disadvantage when it comes to making relationships last: There is always someone else who is quite attractive ready to begin a relationship with them. The intoxicating effects of PEA can return in full force once we begin a relationship with someone new, so we start out our second, third, and fourth relationships with the same illusion—that the attraction will be permanent this time. When the enjoyment doesn't last, we take this development as evidence that we must have chosen incorrectly once again. Focused on this kind of fleeting enjoyment, we can literally search for "true love" our entire lives (see Liebowitz, *The Chemistry of Love*).

Even our attempts to appreciate the body can go awry. I recently saw a magazine advertisement for American Greetings cards that had a copy of an actual greeting card, presumably from Carrie Fisher to her mother, Debbie Reynolds, taped right onto the magazine page. The front of the card said, "If I had a piece of chocolate for every nice thing you do for me . . ." Then on the inside: "I'd have a derriere the size of New Hampshire." Then, as she signed the card, the daughter had written a note to her mother: "Which reminds me—How do you still wear a size 8? Love, Carrie." The note was meant as a compliment. However, of all the compliments this marketing team could have had a daughter give her mother, it seems odd that they identified as the cleverest or most touching one that focused on size. Isn't there so much more to appreciate about another human being than his or her body? And so much more to appreciate about another human being's body than its size?

In an article written to the husbands of women recovering from pregnancy and childbirth, I noted a similar emphasis. To help keep your wife's spirits up, the writer advised, "make vocal and enthusiastic note of every improvement in her figure, no matter how small." Suppose my wife has just had a baby. The process has taken its toll, to be sure. Am I missing the opportunity to marvel at her body's involvement in that experience and to express appreciation for the sacrifices she was willing to make? Too often this is the case, as instead we "make vocal and enthusiastic note" of every step back to looking like a body that shows no signs of having been involved in such a miraculous process.

When my wife, Jenny, was recovering after giving birth to our son Zachary, she became quite ill. She could hardly hold down a meal, and she began losing weight much more quickly than was healthy. At one point her doctor said he might have to hospitalize her and feed her intravenously to insure that she was getting the nutrients she needed. During this time when we were worried for her health, we were constantly amazed at comments from other people about how "fantastic" and "healthy" she looked because she had so quickly lost the weight she put on during her pregnancy. It's scary that in our culture an emaciated and sick body is seen as the picture of health.

Our attempts to appreciate the single, narrow aspect of physical appearance—our own or someone else's—simply do not produce significant, lasting enjoyment. We can see this most clearly in those who take this pursuit to its most extreme form: sex addiction. Those addicts I work with in my clinical practice tend to view people through the filter of sexuality, immediately reducing the women or men they see to sex objects. Not long ago a client described to me what a challenge it was to sit through a church meeting and try not to think about a young woman sitting in front of him. Early in the meeting he had caught a glimpse of her legs through the slit in her dress. From that moment on he vacillated between watching and fantasizing about the young woman and forcing himself to think about other things.

In what ways do you get "stuck" on physical appearance—your own or someone else's? How have you chased your desires in this arena? Are you an appearance addict who has developed a tolerance to the beauty available in your life right now? Have you developed unhealthy habits in an attempt to conform to our culture's sometimes twisted view of health and beauty? Have you permitted yourself to fantasize about bodies you find more attractive than your spouse's? Have you chased desire from one relationship to another in the hopes that this next one will be "the real thing"?

When we get stuck focusing on the physical characteristics of a person when there is so much else to appreciate, we are like a termite in a museum that spends its time chewing on a picture frame, unable to notice that it holds a beautiful Monet landscape. Fortunately, we can take steps to turn from the frame back to the picture—we can shift our attention from sexual attractiveness and instead take in more fully the breadth and depth of other people. We can do so much more to enjoy them, a process we will explore in more depth in a later chapter.

3

We Can Never Get Enough

The world lacks and hankers, and is enslaved to thirst.
—Buddha

What we have seen with regard to possessions and beauty is true of our other desires as well. Their pursuit can be a never-ending process. As we reach a goal, we quickly discover that it is a plateau and not a peak. We mistakenly believed that we would abide when we arrived here, but what we once wanted is not enough, and we move on in the pursuit of more.

Not long ago I was talking with a friend who was about to have laser surgery to correct her vision. I could relate to her excitement because I too am near-sighted. In fact, my vision without contact lenses or glasses is terrible: about 225/20 in my best eye. What an opportunity—*permanent correction of her vision!* What would it be like to wake up in the morning and see clearly from the moment you opened your eyes, we wondered together. No more problems when you went swimming or water-skiing. No more dust particles irritating your contacts, or dry eyes when you rode your bicycle. It sounded wonderful.

"You know that feeling you sometimes get late at night," I asked as we thought about how sweet the change would be for her, "like there's a layer of dirty shag carpet between your eye and your eyelid?"

"Yes, and those eye-watering, pull-over-to-the-side-of-the-road-before-you-crash moments when you are driving," she reminded me.

By the time we had finished our conversation and I was driving home, I was feeling pretty sorry for myself. I had to deal with these irritating contact lenses and I probably would for another few years, at least.

Even from some distance, self-pity is not a pretty thing. As I look back, I realize how twisted my perspective was at that moment. Throughout much of human history, vision problems like mine would have gone uncorrected. I would never have survived as a hunter (where's the beast?) or gatherer (what green stuff?). I remember what a striking difference it made when my optometrist first put those Buddy Holly frames onto my little five-year-old head and asked, "Is that better?" The world was much more vivid and enjoyable when it was in focus. Born as I was in this day and age, not only is my vision corrected but I get to wear these tiny little pieces of plastic right in my eye that make my sight almost perfect. When I first put on contacts—*wow!*—I was amazed to discover that I could see even more clearly. Plus, I could now see even when I went swimming, and there would be no more busted frames from playing basketball or football.

Yet there I was, half a lifetime later, feeling sorry for myself because I had to put up with the very things for which I had once been so grateful.

This is human nature. No matter how good we have it, we can quickly adjust to the status quo. It is easy for our feelings to shift from appreciation to contentment to complacency to entitlement. Then, once we reach entitlement, it's not difficult to take that next step to actual resentment. We feel as if we don't have enough. We want more. We deserve more. We need more, and we shouldn't have to wait for it. These are the seductive lies appetite tells us.

Funny, isn't it, that even though our attempts to establish a solid and final sense of satisfaction have never worked in the past, we don't give up the idea that this illusive goal may be just around the corner. That next big date, the new car, this promotion will really do it. But our date has irritating habits, the car gets a dent, and we discover that working as a manager isn't quite what we had anticipated. Given the regularity and predictability of this process, it's amazing that the futility of escalation doesn't occur to us sooner.

At the end of the movie *Joe versus the Volcano*, Joe and Patricia have just been blasted out to sea by the volcano eruption that destroyed the island of Waponi Woo. They are treading water out in the middle of the ocean when Joe's two luggage crates surface, giving them something to float on. As they discuss the reason they went to the island in the first place, they come to realize that Joe doesn't have a terminal illness after all. "Joe, your whole life is ahead of you!" Patricia says. Joe is not so sure: "We're on a raft, with no land in sight, I don't know." Patricia shakes her head: "It's always going to be *something* with you, isn't it, Joe?"

That response has become a frequently repeated line in my family. We use it to restore perspective whenever we get complaining about how life could be better. "It's always going to be something with you, isn't it, Joe?" The truth is, it's always going to be something with all of us. Even in our relatively safe surroundings and luxurious lives, it's always going to be something.

Considering this predicament, I am reminded of the poetic words of the ancient prophet Isaiah: "It shall even be as when an hungry man dreameth, and, behold, he eateth; but he awaketh, and his soul is empty: or as when a thirsty man dreameth, and, behold, he drinketh; but he awaketh, and, behold, he is faint, and his soul hath appetite" (Isaiah 29:8). No matter how much we have, we will always be capable of desiring more—at least when we remain focused on striving to attain, accrue, and achieve.

Consider your own life: How have you seen your desires escalate? What wishes and hopes have become wants, then necessities, and then aspects of your life that you simply take for granted? What luxuries have become standard equipment at home, in your car, in your lifestyle?

Now take a moment to think about the direction you are going. Do your goals suggest that you've bought into the notion that the answer to finding enjoyment is in escalation? Have you been placing your bets that satisfaction will be yours once you finally have enough money? More achievements? Better possessions? A more fulfilling job? The right relationship?

Appetite's Seductive Lie

Isn't it amazing how a great new lipstick can make your day?
—Radio ad for Clinique makeup

The newspaper ads began running early in the summer: A boy and a girl wearing swimming suits stood in a large yard. On the grass between them sat a sprinkler spraying small streams of water. The girl's arms were folded, her facial expression stern. The boy's shoulders were slumped, and his hands hung at his sides. He looked as though his eyes were about to roll. These kids' body language spoke volumes: They were bored. Disgusted. Fed up. On the verge of exasperation. The caption read, "Maybe this is the year you get the pool."

This cute, memorable ad was part of a marketing campaign for home equity loans. Another in the series showed a snoozing man with a large bug on his nose, captioned: "Been dreaming about adding on a screened porch?" The text of the ads went further: "So why wait any longer to make this summer special? Start enjoying the things you want today."

These messages are so consistent with the way we already think, they hardly strike us as propaganda anymore. "Your kids need more than you're already giving them. You don't want to deprive them of a good, full life. What they need can be purchased with money. And we," the advertisers promise, "will make it easier for you to provide just the right thing."

When we analyze the influence of advertising, we usually think about the way advertisers make us feel about their products. However, consider for a moment the way their messages make us feel about ourselves and our lives. How do you feel toward someone who . . .

- has a spouse who's not as sexy as a model?
- has a headache that lasts more than fifteen minutes?
- has age spots that won't disappear with the application of some cream?
- has a car that doesn't keep out all the noise of the road?

- has to deal with disposable baby diapers that occasionally leak?
- must wait for more than an hour to have an eyeglass prescription filled?
- wears clothing with colors that are less than vivid?

To hear advertisers describe the predicament of these folks, you'd think that they deserve our sympathy, even our pity. It's enough to make us want to take up a collection—until we remind ourselves that *we are* these people whose lives they are portraying as lacking. All of us put up with annoyances such as the ones described above. And yet we are constantly getting the message that no one should have to live with this miserable state of affairs. No wonder we are becoming less and less tolerant of the little daily problems and imperfections in life.

However, advertisers do not *create* the feeling of "not enough" in our lives. They are just capitalizing on it. Promising to pacify it. Pretending they can. The feeling of "not enough" is actually an inherent part of being human. It's a part of the machinery. It may not be constant, but it is recurring.

Advertisers who promise to alleviate the "not enough" state of affairs in our lives are effective only because they have an ally within us. That ally is our appetite. If recruited effectively, our appetite will work overtime for the cause presented to it by advertisers. It is only our own sense of hope, our own neediness, our own desire for delivery from the hard life, the drab life, from *real* life, that can hook us when advertisers cast a line.

Appetite is what tells us just what it would take to get rid of the feeling of "not enough" in our lives. Our deficits quickly transform to desires, and they come with a promise: "Undergo more stimulation or acquire more goods and goodies, and more enjoyment will be yours." Since the feeling of "not enough" is an uncomfortable one, appetite and its accomplices speak with some authority when they promise delivery from it.

To observe just how powerful appetite's propaganda can be, we need look no further than our daily experience. If we take a small taste of ice cream, appetite whispers, "more!" If we ignore its promptings, it may continue to tug at us gently or perhaps even holler in our ear. When we see someone with sex appeal, appetite tells us we must gaze a little longer. When we get a little money, appetite tells us we must have more. It always tells us that we are on the right track but must continue along. And our reward for continuing, appetite implies, will be lasting satisfaction. Appetite's seductive lie is that if we attain what it drives us to seek, it will be enough. We have an immediate sense that, "this next bite (or boyfriend) will really do it for me." Satisfaction is just around the corner now.

It is clear from the tactics companies use to lure potential customers that they have learned how appetite works. Stores give out free samples of tasty snack foods. Even the sight of a steak being turned on the grill and the sound of its sizzle can be enough to beckon us on. Previews for movies or TV shows will "tease" viewers by providing a taste of the excitement to come.

Although our appetite and its accomplices deliver a convincing sales pitch, reality refuses to honor the bargain. As we have seen again and again, increased stimulation and acquisition quite often fail to fulfill us. In fact, instead of making us enjoy our lives more, they typically leave us less and less able to feel satisfied.

Wouldn't you think reality would break the spell? It seems as if we would be more skeptical once appetite has left us standing at the altar a time or two. However, even after we've seen through appetite's propaganda, even after we have realized that it fails miserably to keep its promises, it will not give up the game. The spell appetite casts is a potent one, and it won't relinquish its captives easily. Its messages are still very convincing—even compelling—when it strikes. The amazing and ironic truth is that appetite, in spite of the fact that it lies to us, still manages to seduce us time after time.

I have learned about appetite's tenacious hold, its persistent power to persuade, most powerfully in my work with psychotherapy clients like Oliver. He doesn't enjoy food like he used to: "Now I just eat to survive. I don't really care what it tastes like." And, he confides, "Sex is not enjoyable, either, hasn't been for years." He doesn't particularly care for music, dancing, or socializing beyond casual conversation. Talking with Oliver, you soon begin to wonder, what keeps him going? What makes his life worth living? Enjoyment, to a great extent, has escaped him.

He makes and refinishes cabinets for a living. Every now and then the smell of freshly cut wood rekindles a hint of pleasure. It is somewhat gratifying for him to look over a piece of work he has just completed. And he feels a bit of satisfaction when he gets a new client. Once in a while, a holiday or other special occasion brings a sense of warmth to his heart. But most of the time, he wades day after day through an emotional desert. The official label for the symptom he suffers is *anhedonia*, meaning that he has difficulty finding pleasure in what should be enjoyable activities. This ailment did not strike randomly or from out of the blue. Oliver has an opiate addiction that has come to interfere with his capacity for pleasure.

In his early twenties, Oliver was drafted into the military and stationed overseas. He soon discovered that just about everyone at his military base used a chemical of some kind to escape. "Almost every night, the older men, mostly officers, went to the canteen to get drunk. The younger crowd of enlisted men I hung out with taught me to shoot up," he explained.

After his discharge from the military, Oliver faced all kinds of challenges as he tried to readjust to civilian life. When the opportunity to use heroin again arose, it provided a welcome relief, an escape from the complexities and ambiguities of the life he was trying to piece together. He used the drug on and off for twelve years, trying to stop at times and going on long runs of escalating use at others.

Oliver was locked in a downward spiral. Like every other individual who has used heroin extensively, he had reached the point of diminishing returns. When he went for even a few hours without shooting up, he felt anxious and irritable. His muscles ached and started to cramp. His body would slam back and forth between cold chills and hot sweats. He couldn't sleep at all at night. Within less than a day, his nose and eyes were dripping and he could feel his heart pounding against the inside of his rib cage.

Oliver knew he had to get out of this spiral. He had had enough of a life that revolved around obtaining, hiding, using, and recovering from the effects of the drug. He promised himself "never again." Nonetheless, when he set limits and goals, they typically failed to change things for long. In the throes of withdrawal one night, he called the hospital emergency room in desperation. He now hated his habit and wanted to stop for good, but he realized he couldn't do it on his own. They referred him to the city's methadone clinic.

Methadone is a narcotic, but it doesn't lead to a "high" like heroin or morphine. And it stays in the system longer, so it can be taken just once a day, unlike heroin, which leaves its users craving within hours. Oliver stayed on the "methadone maintenance" program and has been getting his daily dose for the last seven years.

Even on methadone, avoiding illicit drug use has not been easy, and several times during his treatment Oliver has relapsed for brief periods. One morning during my work with him, Oliver walked into my office at the clinic clearly upset. He had just witnessed a drug deal in the parking lot. His description of this experience drove home to me just how potent appetite's propaganda can be. In spite of all the years he had lost to heroin, in spite of all it had cost him in money, energy, and pain for himself and his family, his witnessing the exchange of the drug had sent a tidal wave of temptation over him. Amazingly enough, in spite of the lies appetite had told him before, that morning its message was just as convincing as ever!

Fortunately, a part of him held on to the knowledge that his urges were deceiving him. He came immediately in to see me for strength, for reinforcement. As we talked, his resolve to stay clean returned and his rationality was firmly reestablished. But his battle was not over. He and I both knew that when the wrong circumstances combined with the wrong state of mind, the threat of using again would return. Oliver had had friends at the clinic who had been killed by their drug habit. Some had lost custody of their children, and a couple had even lost their children to death due to drug-related neglect. But even the threat of the worst consequences imaginable makes little difference for Oliver when the compulsion to use takes over again. That is how persuasive appetite's appeal to us can be.

Which of appetite's lies are you seduced by most frequently?

How much power are you giving appetite's accomplices in your life? You can combat this by becoming more aware of how your appetite is stimulated by the advertising you take in. Instead of acting immediately on your urges to buy, you may want to try keeping a wish list and buying only those items that have been on the list for a month. You'll be amazed at how your desire for many seeming necessities dwindles once the effect of advertising has had a chance to fade. Shield yourself from television, radio, newspaper, and magazine advertising for a time and see if your "needs" start to diminish. A camping trip may be a good opportunity to try this. You may even decide to take a media "fast."

5 The Intensity Trap

He who knows not when he has enough is poor.
—Japanese proverb

Imagine that a friend has come seeking your help, complaining that she no longer enjoys life. The well of passion has run dry for her. She is bored and dissatisfied, and would like your suggestions for breaking out of this monotonous, dull existence. What advice would you give her? What is the solution to the emptiness she is experiencing? How can she overcome her lack of enjoyment?

One day I gave a class full of students in a graduate business class the above scenario. Here are the suggestions they offered:

- Start a new hobby
- Take an exotic getaway
- Buy a new CD
- Do something to spice up your love life
- Try out bungee jumping, rock climbing, hang gliding, or some other high-adrenaline sport
- Go shopping
- Go dancing

These suggestions, like most I hear when I ask for input on this kind of "problem," entail some kind of increase in stimulation. Since what we already have is not "doing it" for us, we try to throw another log on the fire to turn up the heat. We do this because we believe appetite's promise that *having* more will *do* more for us.

However, as we explored in the previous chapter, when we pursue it rabidly, satisfaction is rarely ours for long; it seems to slip away quickly and remain just out of reach. No matter how far we jack up the intensity, our appetite simply rises to just above whatever new level we have reached. Because of this, stimulation must be constantly increased to match our voracious appetites.

This is the nature of the intensity trap, and it can escalate into what I have labeled "the cycle of addiction" in the image on the next page. Even as we pursue and seek it, satisfaction eludes us because our needs expand at an even quicker rate.

Appetite is forever exceeding stimulation's expansion because enjoyment's physical and spiritual machinery are damaged once they are bombarded and overloaded. The body's natural pleasure chemicals make everyday life interesting and enjoyable. However, this exquisite system is also a delicate one. It provides us the *capacity* to enjoy life, but its existence by no means guarantees that it will forever operate optimally. In fact, our enjoyment system operates on a "use it *wisely* or lose it" basis, just as so many of our other capacities do. People who flood their pleasure systems with intense stimulation essentially overload the circuits, spoiling to some extent their future capacity to enjoy the more natural doses that result from what once were enjoyable activities.

We pay a long-term, sometimes permanent price for immediate rewards that are artificially or improperly induced. Substances and behaviors become addictive precisely to the extent that they trigger or mimic the body's own chemicals and activate our natural reward system. It is an emotional jolt, and can be a "thrill," to take our bodies, which are finely tuned to respond to the nuances and subtleties of the most minute stimulation, and subject them to stimulation that overwhelms. Our auditory system, which can bring us sublime enjoyment in response to a simple chord progression strummed out on a guitar, can also make our hearts race and adrenaline flow in reaction to the jolts and screeches of "music" that assaults. The same sexual responsiveness sensitive enough that we can appreciate a soft touch or the mere sight of our spouse can also be overloaded by the sight of sculpted bodies in provocative poses. The same neural circuits that provide twinges of empathy when we witness a child scraping her knee will also provide a chest-pounding, gut-wrenching,

DEPRIVATION

Cycle of
ENJOYMENT

APPRECIATION

WORKING
AND WAITING

DESIRES,
APPETITES,
CRAVINGS

DESIRES,
APPETITES,
CRAVINGS

DESIRES,
APPETITES,
CRAVINGS

DISSATISFACTION

INDULGING

Cycle of
ADDICTION

IMMEDIATE
GRATIFICATION

sweaty-palmed thrill if we subject ourselves to filmed scenes of violent horror or action.

All of these overpowering methods will work to provide the bodily responses associated with emotion. You can use a Stradivarius as a tennis racket, too, but the fact that it will do the job temporarily doesn't make that a good idea. A fine violin might return a lob or two and perhaps even survive a backhand smash, but the overall effect in terms of its intended purpose would be to ruin an instrument that might have otherwise lasted lifetimes. Similarly, the payoff gained through deliberate emotional overloading evaporates almost immediately into thin air.

In a healthy courtship, for instance, the subtle stimulation of affectionate touch is pleasurable and inviting. A desire for increasing intimacy, when pursued intelligently and with restraint, can draw a couple to ever-deepening levels of commitment and enjoyment of each other's company. But the same vehicle that, if not abused, can eventually transport the couple to an entire world of wondrous destinations can also be hijacked and exploited for joy-riding. Once it has been used for thrill-seeking, however, transforming it back so that it fits for its original purpose is not nearly as quick or simple a process.

One of the reasons we develop a tolerance for stimulation and become desensitized is that the body doesn't ignore the state of excess we create when we indulge. Like a thermostat that turns off the furnace when the house is warm enough, feedback mechanisms in the body shut down production of these internal pleasure messengers as the system is flooded. After we subject ourselves to an artificially intense degree of stimulation, we becomes increasingly insensitive to such stimulation, and the intensity must be increased even more to have the same effect. Eventually, forget about ecstasy, the addicted individual can't even feel *normal* without the excessive behavior or the drug. This is the paradoxical nature of the cycle of addiction: We add more and more stimulation only to find that it does less and less for us.

Sebastian Junger described the thrill of leaving the safety of American society to work as a journalist in Croatia during the height of the Balkan conflict. After spending time on the battle front near Sarajevo, he headed south to a town called Split. "What surprised me . . . given what a [coward] I thought I had been about the dangers in Sarajevo, was how dull life suddenly seemed without them. In Split, we were able to cross the road without a second thought, to sit at a cafe and order a wonderful meal—and suddenly everything felt drab and dead. Nothing was exciting; nothing was worth doing. All I wanted was to go back to that strange city where everything I did seemed big and important and was, potentially, the last act of my life" ("The Lure of Danger," 57). The effect of addiction is similar to the effect experienced by that journalist. Whenever the body adjusts down its internal mechanisms in response to overload, our sensitivity to stimulation shrinks, along with our ability to enjoy it.

When the original amount of substance or level of behavior no longer produces the same effect, we say that an addict in this bind has developed a "tolerance." The same amount provides less satisfaction, so the alcoholic's drink of choice changes from beer to vodka, the pornography addict moves on to an affair, and the gambler quits work altogether to spend more time trying to recover losses. But even with increased stimulation, the cycle must continue because we reap ever less enjoyment from the stimulation we do experience. Because we are now less sensitive to and aware of stimulation, we find that we suffer increasingly from dissatisfaction with life and from boredom. Then, once again, in an attempt to escape this dreariness, we raise the level of intensity, and the cycle begins another turn.

When we act as though the intensity or quality of stimulation is the key to enjoying life, we lock ourselves in a vicious circle and become like dogs chasing our tails. Instead of more enjoyment, our tactic leads to less. Yesterday's titillating pin-up poster becomes today's magazine ad, and today's thrilling blockbuster becomes tomorrow's yawner. Whenever an activity is pursued for the sheer thrill of it, it seems that in that very indulgence we lose some of our capacity to be thrilled, and even our capacity to enjoy generally. We become ever more callused and hard to please.

In her book A *Return to Modesty*, Wendy Shalit describes a particularly fascinating illustration of the intensity trap and its long-term effect. She compared photographs of men and women on public beaches at the turn of the twentieth century with photographs from modern nude beaches. The playful glances exchanged by the women and men in the old photographs convey a sense of attraction and excitement, she notes, while the nudists appear bored and distracted.

Looking back, one can imagine how the logic of escalation operated. If an exposed ankle was intriguing, suits that showed the calf must have provided twice the thrill. The excitement that came with each new step did not last, however, and we have had to "progress" all the way to see-through fabrics and thong bikinis. Shalit's prescription: Return to modesty and soon less will become more again.

The "hungry ghost" is the personification Tibetan Buddhists give to our cravings. The insatiable nature of these cravings is symbolized by a creature with a gigantic belly and a very tiny throat. As a result, it can always be consuming and still remain voraciously hungry. The more the ghost eats, the larger grows its belly and the smaller its throat (see Muller, *Sabbath*, 126). This is how our abundance has turned to scarcity, how our overflowing lives leave us feeling empty.

Unfortunately, most of us are well on our way down this deadening path. The breadth and depth of our desensitization are astounding. Both as individuals and as a society, we have subjected ourselves to an improper and artificially intense level of stimulation that has deadened our senses and our sensibilities. We are left demanding more stimulation than ever in order to achieve enjoyment. This "cycle of addiction" is a vicious circle, a trap into which we once set foot voluntarily and now find ourselves stuck.

Fortunately, the intensity trap still allows us some wiggle-room, and we can liberate ourselves if we are willing to put in the effort. The first step for us is to recognize the ways in which we have been chasing desire and thereby raising our appetite one notch at a time to new levels. Are you still believing appetite's propaganda in some areas of your life? Do you believe that more intensity is what you need in your work? In your love life? In the activities you pursue during your leisure time and in your entertainment choices?

We can begin to emerge from our bondage by refusing to continue to escalate the intensity of these pursuits. Then we will gradually recover from our current state of "too much" and be better prepared to enjoy hunger's hidden treasures.

The Age of Addiction

There is no greater disaster than greed.
—Lao-tzu

The longer I work with people who are addicted, the more I realize that, unfortunately, their pathology is not as unusual as I once assumed. The destructive process of addiction characterizes what is going on all around us. Desensitization has come to permeate our culture and is creeping into all of our lives. It is instructive to consider cases of addiction because the process of narrowing interests and deadening sensibilities operates the same way for all of us. Some addicts merely travel further and more quickly down the devastating path. Having been where we are headed, they hold up to us warning signs about the nature of our final destination. My hope is that those warning signs will finally convince us to do a 180-degree turn and reverse the process of desensitization in our lives.

Since we are concerned about the effect of the cycle of addiction not only upon us as individuals but on our society, one of the most informative "cases" we can study is that of a culture that traveled quite far down the path of desensitization. Therefore, we will be considering in some detail the ancient Roman Empire's use of violence for entertainment. If your interest is sparked by this discussion, I highly recommend the video *The True Story of the Roman Arena*, from which I gathered much of the information I will summarize below.

For the Romans near the meridian of time, violence was not just a means of building their empire but a form of celebration. At the funerals of important men, they staged gladiator duels in which two prisoners fought to the death, with the survivor earning his freedom. The blood of the loser, it was believed, appeased the spirit of the deceased dignitary. Over time, competing politicians tried to outdo each other with bigger and more spectacular contests at the funerals of statesmen and military leaders. Witnessing the crowds' enthusiasm for these battles, perhaps Julius Caesar saw their expansion as a way to build his own popularity. Or maybe he valued the blurring of individual identities into a frenzied mass that cheered on its favorite contender as a potential vehicle for building cohesiveness that could be channeled into patriotism. Whatever his reasons, in 40 B.C. Caesar broke with tradition and held the first "games" independent of a funeral. He put on a match in memory of his daughter who had died nine years earlier.

Once they were no longer dependent on the death of a public figure, the games could be held at the convenience of the rulers, and could be planned in advance for greatest effect. Gradually the games expanded in size and in drama, growing from battles between small groups of gladiators in an amphitheater to the eventual day-long events filled with increasingly extreme and bizarre spectacles. People were tied up as prey to animals, animals were slaughtered by the hundreds, captive children were made to fight, as were women, dwarves, and blind prisoners. The size of the crowds grew, and so larger and larger venues had to be built to accommodate them. Coming into power after this foundation had been laid, Augustus fed the people's growing appetite, and the games thrived during his reign. Eventually, during the reign of Titus and at the pinnacle of the era, the massive Coliseum, one of the most impressive architectural structures ever, was erected to hold the games. Not only was the Coliseum the center of the city but the games quickly became the focal point of Roman culture, eclipsing people's attention to politics, religion, and milder forms of entertainment.

The violence of the games had a desensitizing effect on those who witnessed them, as described by St. Augustine:

> *When he saw the blood, it was like drinking in a deep draught of savage passion. Rather than turn away, he fixed his eyes on the scene and took in all its frenzy, unaware of what he was doing. He reveled in the wickedness of the fighting, grew*

intoxicated with the bloodshed. When he left the arena, he took with him a sick mind, which would leave him no peace until he came back again, no longer as one of the group which had first dragged him there, but as their leader, taking new sheep to the slaughter.

To the rulers' surprise and sometimes even their disgust, the people's bloodlust grew and their enthusiasm for the shows could not be maintained without almost constant escalations in "quality" and quantity. Even brief pauses in the action bored the crowd, so a complicated labyrinth of tunnels, descending three and four stories beneath ground level, was constructed so that animals and warriors could be brought onto and removed from the field with minimal interruption. Spectacles that would have horrified the citizens at first exposure became commonplace, and the crowds demanded even more. The rulers quickly discovered, however, that their attempts to increase the drama and novelty of the games could not keep pace with the people's growing appetite. They pressured judges to pass sentences of death simply to provide more prisoners to execute, thus making for a day that was gory enough to please the citizens. Rulers spared no expense to bring exotic animals in for the slaughter.

Interestingly, the desensitizing effect of witnessing these displays was not limited to the citizens' tolerance of violence only. Rather, their moral degradation occurred in a comprehensive way, as evidenced by the fact that prostitutes crowded under the arches around the arena at the end of the day to await the crowds who had just had their spirits numbed and emotions agitated. The poet Seneca, who said that "Nothing is more damaging than wasting time at the games," observed this comprehensive deadening of spiritual and social sensitivities in his own reaction to them: "It is then that vice steals secretly upon you, through the avenue of pleasure. I return home more greedy, ambitious, even more cruel and inhumane because I have been with human beings."

Cicero, a member of the Roman Senate, could see the direction his society was headed, and raised a voice of warning:

> *The daily spectacle of atrocious acts has stifled all feeling of pity in the hearts of men. When every hour we see or hear of an act of dreadful cruelty we lose all feeling of humanity. Crime no longer horrifies us. We smile at the enormities of our youth. We condone passion, when we should understand that the unrestrained emotions of men produce chaos. Once we were a nation of self-control and austerity, and had a reverence for life and justice. This is no longer true. We prefer our politicians, particularly if they swagger with youth and are accomplished jesters and liars. We love entertainment, even in law and government. Unless we reform our fate is terrible.* (Caldwell, A Pillar of Iron, 322)

Ultimately, the Roman rulers could not support the habit they helped create. They could no longer put on a show that topped the last one, and the people were no longer content to settle for less. The system, dependent upon ever-escalating intensity, collapsed in upon itself when the upper limit was reached. The games died out, the final event being held in 549 A.D.

A myriad of sociological factors intermingled, and it may be impossible to determine what role each played in the decline and eventual fall of the Roman Empire. Nonetheless, lessons can be drawn regarding the desensitizing effect of the violence on Roman culture. As *London Times* political columnist Ronald Butt has summarized: "The history of the Roman arena instructs us how the appetite of a people can be created by what is fed to it—the upper classes of Rome were systematically addicted by their rulers to the frenzy and titillation of sadistic violence by a steady progression from less to more until the Roman character itself was conditioned to a course of insensibility to suffering" (Maxwell, *Deposition*, 17).

It is tempting to view the desensitization that afflicted the ancient inhabitants of the Roman Empire as an aberration, a historical anomaly. We might prefer to dismiss the cycle of addiction as something that occurs in our day only in the lives of skid-row addicts or hardened criminals. The fact is, the Roman culture's escalating tolerance demonstrates the paradoxical effect that intense stimulation, gratification, and indulgence have on enjoyment, and the end result is not unique to a particular time or place or people. The same process of diminishing returns operates whenever people violate their own nature by pursuing appetite's call for an ever-increasing intensity.

Unfortunately, we live in a time where the operation of the cycle of addiction and the resulting hardening of hearts can be seen all around us. There is more stimulation available than ever before. More marriages end in divorce due to boredom, more people say that their lives lack excitement, and more people complain about their work than perhaps ever before. While we as a society may not yet be as hardened as the Romans became, we are headed in that direction.

Columnist Karl Taro Greenfeld has noted that Americans who find everyday life too dull have "embarked on a national orgy of thrill seeking and risk taking. The rise of adventure and extreme sports . . . is the most vivid manifestation of this new national behavior. . . . Even our social behavior has tilted toward the treacherous, with unprotected sex on the upswing and hard drugs like heroin the choice of the chic as well as the junkies" ("Life on the Edge," 30).

As with the ancient Romans, our own society's entertainment options provide an index of our deterioration into a cycle of addiction. Anyone who watches daytime TV has had paraded before him or her person after person with outrageously deviant lifestyles. Those who watch in prime time will find themselves witnessing more and more violence, more and more sex. It is not necessary for viewers to embrace these aberrations in order for such programming to have a desensitizing effect. The exposure alone will lead to a sort of habituation of attitude—what we are used to seeing automatically becomes less unusual to us.

Television advertisers have also become caught in this cycle of intensification. The purpose of most advertising is not to inform but to stimulate just enough to create an appetite for more. The problem is that future ads must up the ante in order to have the same power. As a result, we now have television spots that burst dozens of images in rapid-fire succession onto the screen with music blaring in the background.

Roger C. Schlobin of Purdue University has suggested an innovative barometer of desensitization by comparing the volume and intensity of disturbing content in popular films with that found in their sequels. He has pointed out, for example, that the violence in *The Amityville Horror, Poltergeist, Jaws, Friday the 13th, Nightmare on Elm Street,* and *Alien* is exceeded in each case by that of their sequels. Schlobin asserts that fans "constantly crave gorier and gorier sequels . . . to awaken dulled tastes and sensibilities. Such well-schooled respondents respond with yawns to effects that will give innocents nightmares for weeks" ("Children of a Darker God," 25–50).

Television and movies are not the only media culprits. Analyzing the effects that violent video games have on children, Colonel Johnston Beach, a psychology professor at West Point, said: "I think kids have adapted themselves to a much higher level of stimulation. They have to do more to get excited, which just makes it more likely that people will go out and do stupid things." In our day we are certainly witnessing some of the "stupid things" people end up doing when they have allowed their appetite for vice to run rampant.

A primary reason our entertainment gets more and more degrading over time is that writers, producers, and advertisers are now faced with the task of trying to stimulate adults who have ingested massive amounts of programming from daily consumption that has spanned the decades of their lives. Needless to say, it takes more to catch such consumers' interest, let alone to excite them at all. So the entertainment industry has obliged and given us more—not more quality, but more intensity. And by so doing they take one more step downward in a vicious spiral.

The watch group Parents Television Council has painstakingly documented the gradual decline of standards as TV audiences have become more callused and harder to please. In fall 1999 the group released a study titled "The Family Hour: Worse Than Ever and Headed for New Lows." In the year and a half that had elapsed since their previous study, the investigators noted a significant rise in objectionable material in all three of the categories they tracked: foul language, references to sexual activity, and depictions of violence. Objectionable material was noted to occur at an average rate of seven incidents per hour of programming, a rate that was up 75 percent from the previous study, with violent content nearly doubling during that time. The authors concluded by previewing the next programming season, describing it as "likely to be the foulest fall lineup in the history of television."

Of course, this perspective was offered by a group with an obvious agenda and, some might even argue, a vendetta. Were they overreacting, painting the picture as more bleak than it actually is? Surprisingly enough, many of the Hollywood elite agree with their portrayal. By contrast, however, most of them see nothing wrong with it, and in fact many welcome the changes. "It's where we should be headed. It's the millennium, come on, let's get with it!" exclaimed *Ally McBeal* star Greg Germann on an interview televised on *Entertainment Tonight*. Camryn Manheim, who stars in *The Practice*, concurred: "I'm all against censorship, so whatever's pushing the limits is all right by me." *Spin City's* Michael Boatman expressed hope that such changes would continue: "I don't think that there's actually enough pushing of the envelope, and I would love to see the networks follow the cable networks." More than hopeful, Jay Mohr, star of the series *Action*, offered a prediction: "As far as pushing the envelope, the line is going to move every year, it's going to get lower every year" (Parents Television Council, "e-Alerts").

Personally, I found the perspective expressed by these entertainers to be chilling, a sad commentary on our day. We treat the lowering of standards as a moral obligation and then, as our consciences darken, we congratulate ourselves on being more enlightened. Entertainers may claim that they "push the envelope" of acceptability out of artistic merit or as champions of free expression, but I have a hunch that many of them know very well that their survival depends on turning up the stimulation level a notch to match the "needs" of their desensitized viewers. The problem is that there is no easy exit from this spiral. Even as I write this, I'm sure that viewers are becoming bored with the "sizzling" new schedule, finding content that would have been considered too much not long ago is no longer even enough.

Have you noticed the increase in degrading content on television, at the theater, in magazines, and in other media? If so, have you taken steps to remove yourself from its effect? Are you floating along with the flow of popular culture, or are you and your family determining your own course? Those of us who have not noticed the gradual decline in media quality and standards should perhaps be the most concerned—we may be the most entangled in the grasp of intensity's trap.

When the Machinery Is Out of Order

Nothing is enough for the man to whom enough is too little.
—Epicurus

Some people aren't thrilled as easily as others. They complain of boredom and feel understimulated much of the time. They may seek out risks that seem beyond daring to the rest of us.

You won't typically find these people spending hours on end reading or daydreaming. Nor are you likely to find them strolling through museums or working at desk jobs. They prefer the active life, and their wanderlust can lead them from job to job, from city to city, and often from spouse to spouse.

Although such a condition may develop in a few as they act in ways that desensitize them, many elements of it can also be inborn. Scientific investigation of individuals who suffer this kind of biologically based enjoyment deficit is yielding valuable lessons about how the process of enjoyment normally works.

Neuropharmacologist Kenneth Blum gave the label "reward deficiency syndrome" to the cluster of symptoms I have begun to describe. He has explored the biological correlates to this psychological and behavioral state of affairs. His investigation has led him to link the syndrome to an underresponsiveness in the reward or pleasure centers of the body. His research has also verified that individuals who suffer from this kind of insensitivity are at increased risk of abusing drugs and alcohol. They are also more likely to develop compulsive behavior of other kinds. He surmises that such people are attempting to correct through their behavior an imbalance in an internal system (see Blum et al., "Reward Deficiency Syndrome," 132–45).

As a counselor in the field of addictions, I have worked with several clients suffering from this kind of reward deficiency. One was a sixteen-year-old boy named Carl. Carl's parents were desperate; they were willing to try anything they thought might help the boy. One month before I met him, he had emerged from a hospital chemical dependency treatment program. It had been his third time through. Unfortunately, both of the previous times, he had quickly returned to his old ways. In spite of the fact that he had "graduated" from the program this last time through, his follow-up drug test had just come up positive for amphetamines. That was when his mother called me.

I agreed to see Carl but was skeptical about my ability to help him. When Carl came to my office with his family, I was immediately surprised by his demeanor. He displayed none of the telltale signs of teenage rebellion: no defiant posture or stare, no bizarre hair style, no outlandish clothing. Instead, here was a young man who discussed his drug and alcohol problem quite candidly. He had gone back to drinking, he admitted, and had done it "for the buzz." He found the town we lived in boring. He didn't enjoy family activities. He found schoolwork intolerable and couldn't read more than a couple of sentences at a time without feeling dazed and sleepy.

As I talked with Carl, I realized that he didn't drink for the usual reasons. Most alcoholics tend to drink alcohol for its calming effect. However, there is another, smaller group that drinks for self-stimulation (Cloninger, "Neurogenetic Adaptive Mechanisms in Alcoholism," 410–16). These folks tend to drink more, in part because it takes more alcohol to stimulate than it does to soothe. They also are more likely to abuse uppers like amphetamines and cocaine than anti-anxiety drugs and tranquilizers. This subclass of alcoholics is also more likely to engage in antisocial behavior.

The people most likely to engage in antisocial behavior are those who fall at the far end of the insensitivity spectrum. For decades Robert Hare of the University of British Columbia has been investigating people in this group whose antisocial behavior is so extreme that it characterizes their personality—those diagnosed as psychopaths. Hare has discovered a pattern of underarousal that appears connected to these criminals' difficulty in learning from their mistakes. Psychopaths about to receive an electric shock, for instance, don't show the signs of fear that most people do (Goleman, *Emotional Intelligence*, 109–10).

In another study, scrambled words were flashed on a screen and subjects had to decipher them. Some words were emotionally neutral, such as *chair*. It took psychopaths and control subjects about the same length of time to decipher these words, and the brain-wave responses of both groups were also similar. However, when the scrambled word that flashed on the screen was emotionally loaded, such as *kill*, a difference in the two groups emerged. The normal subjects deciphered these words more quickly and displayed an aroused brain-wave response—clearly, an emotional "button" had been pushed. This emotional "button," however, turned out to be lacking in the psychopaths. They deciphered the word *kill* no more quickly than a neutral word, nor did they display a distinctive brain-wave response. This deficit in the capacity to generate emotion-linked bodily responses interferes with psychopaths' ability to experience their own emotions. By extension, of course, it may also be a factor that prevents them from empathizing with others (Goleman, *Emotional Intelligence*, 109–10).

My client Carl displayed to a milder degree the bodily underresponsiveness that was common to the psychopaths studied by Hare. In fact, during our first meeting, he described an incident that illustrates this symptom in a striking way. He said that he was out joy-riding with his buddies. The driver of the car went around a hairpin turn too fast, and the car skidded out of control. By the time his friend was able to regain control and stop the vehicle, they had come dangerously close to going off the road and over the edge of an embankment. Carl said that his three other friends in the car had been panic-stricken by the incident. He looked over and saw that the one sitting next to him was shaking so badly that there were ripples in the drink in his cup. Carl looked down at his own drink—no ripples—and he noticed that, oddly enough, he didn't feel scared, either.

Fortunately, relatively recent scientific findings have led to the development of EEG biofeedback, a method that in many cases can partially correct biological deficits like Carl's. I had been researching EEG biofeedback as a potential means of addressing the desensitization that occurs with addiction. Because Carl's insensitivity preceded and seemed to be the fuel upon which his addiction fed, I told his parents that the method might be worth a try. I referred them to Fran Bryson, a biofeedback practitioner in Rigby, Idaho.

The treatment's effect on Carl was profound. Academic work that he had once found intolerable became somewhat less tedious to him. His moods became more manageable, and his outbursts at home decreased in frequency and intensity. Most notably, his satisfaction with everyday life gradually increased, and he was no longer as dependent on drugs or alcohol to make life interesting and exciting.

Last time I spoke with Carl's mother, she told me he had recently had a "slip": He used marijuana while on a fishing trip with his buddies. His struggle to stay clean and sober is an ongoing one. Nonetheless, his life is certainly more manageable—and enjoyable—than it was.

I was sufficiently inspired by what I saw with Carl to do a brief apprenticeship with Fran and obtain the equipment and training necessary to add the technique to my own repertoire. I have seen similar results with a majority—but by no means all—of my clients who suffer from reward deficiency syndrome. Unfortunately, I have not yet seen any evidence, either in my own work or in the scientific literature, that the method can lessen at all the severe underarousal displayed by psychopaths.

It is impossible to discern the relative effects of biology, environment, and life choices in determining a given individual's capacity for enjoyment. It is clear, nonetheless, that some people begin life with a relatively compromised physical reactivity and a blunted emotional responsiveness.

This affects a number of areas of their lives, most notably their emotional life, their ability to empathize, their conscience, and their ability to enjoy the stimulation they normally experience. Too many of us, unlike people suffering from an inborn deficiency, are responsible ourselves for most of the dumbing-down of our own enjoyment quotient. Our enjoyment system is not a static and stable one, but is dynamic and responsive. It reacts to the life experiences we choose by, in turn, making changes of its own.

The reactive nature of our enjoyment's machinery was verified in a research study I participated in as a young boy. My brother, Brent, and I were recruited because we were part of a relatively unique group: Our family didn't own a TV set. One day when I was about seven, my mom picked us up early from school and drove us from our suburban town to the campus of a nearby university. After a brief wait in a reception area, Brent was led down a hallway while Mom and I waited. After a while he returned, and I was then taken down the hallway and into a dimly lit room and seated in a large, comfortable chair that faced a screen. The people there talked to me briefly as they taped some wires to my skin. They then started a movie and let me watch for a while. I vaguely recall watching someone ski down a mountain. After a few minutes they unhooked the wires and led me back to where Mom and Brent were waiting.

I will never forget what happened as we walked back out to the car. Mom took out two five-dollar bills and handed one to each of us. She said the money was ours for coming in to help these folks with the work they were doing. We were amazed and delighted. It would have taken us months to save up that amount by doing chores around the house. That was the first time I had ever held that much money in my hand. This was not a bad deal: Sit down and watch some TV, then get paid for it. I was ready to come back the next day and "help them" again!

Much later Mom explained that we had taken part in a study by psychologist Victor Cline on the desensitizing effects of television. She had responded to an advertisement in the newspaper requesting the involvement of children who had not watched much TV. As part of the group who had not been exposed to much television, we were compared with a group who were more used to watching TV.

More recently, as I delved more deeply into my own study of desensitization, I returned to the university to view the scientific report of Dr. Cline's study for myself. There, in a worn volume with yellowing pages, I found the article, only six pages long, titled "Desensitization of Children to Television Violence."

Sure enough, two minutes' worth of ski footage was shown. Although I could not remember it, we had also watched a chase scene (from the W. C. Fields movie *The Bank Dick*) and a boxing match from the movie *The Champion*. Later when I asked my mom she verified it: "Because of that we wondered whether or not we had done the right thing, subjecting you to that experiment." I reassured her, "It was science, Mom. You were furthering the cause of science!"

The wires they had taped to our skin were measuring our physiological response to the movie scenes—our "blood volume pulse amplitude" and our skin conductance or "galvanic skin response." To put it more simply, they wanted to see how fast and hard our hearts beat and how much we sweat. Basically, the researchers were interested in how aroused we were by the footage they showed.

Dr. Cline and his colleagues discovered that our group was sensitive to violence. We were responsive. Our bodies and emotions were readily and rapidly aroused by the boxing scenes. By contrast, the "high-exposure-to-TV" group showed notably lower levels of arousal when watching the violent scenes. When it came to the ski movie, we showed no more arousal than the regular television viewers had, demonstrating that it was not simply watching an action-packed scene that had triggered our unusual response. Rather, Dr. Cline concluded that, with the help of television, the nervous systems of the "high-exposure" children had become a little less sensitive. Having viewed more televised violence in their lifetimes, they had become more accustomed to it. Even at that tender age, kids in that group had been desensitized. Without intending to, their parents had allowed these kids to subject themselves to stimulation that was moving them in small but perceptible—even tangible and physically measurable—increments in the direction of the insensitivity that is shown by psychopaths.

Our ability to correct inborn imbalances in our enjoyment quotient remains limited. However, we must not lose sight of the fact that most damage to enjoyment's machinery results from experiences and choices, and the prevention of this damage remains within our control.

How sensitive are you to the varieties of stimulation that can fuel enjoyment? Has this degree of sensitivity remained constant? Have you ever enjoyed life more fully than you do now? Look back at family pictures from when you were a toddler. How much pleasure did you take in life then? What about during your childhood, adolescence, or young adulthood? If you discover that you have become desensitized over time, you'll be glad to know that we will now be turning our attention to the dynamic process of expanding our capacity for enjoyment.

PART II

Expanding
Enjoyment

Coming to Our Senses

Nothing can cure the soul but the senses, just as nothing can cure the senses but the soul.
—Oscar Wilde

It begins at birth—perhaps even before—and can continue through-out our lives: Our finely tuned physiology enables us to enjoy exquisitely ourselves and the world that surrounds us. Anyone who has ever watched a crying newborn soothed as she sucks at her mother's breast will agree: Her enjoyment of life has begun! We are not left only to our imagina-tions. We can also use the ebb and flow of the body's enjoyment chemicals as a window into the experience of these little ones. Indeed, these chem-icals respond to all sorts of experiences in babies just as they do in adults. Certain forms of stimulation have been shown to release endorphins and increase the activity of the pleasure chemical dopamine in the brains of infants, tipping us off that the touch of a loved one, to use one example, can be as soothing to these tiny ones as it can to us adults.

In an effort to discover how narcotics like morphine and opiates like heroin affect the human brain, maverick brain scientist Candace Pert and her colleagues at the National Institute of Mental Health in the 1970s went looking for an opiate receptor in the human brain. When her seniors were ready to abandon the project, Pert, a young graduate student at the time, drove on, immersing herself in the work. Sleepless nights and marathon weekends in the lab paid off when eventually she discovered the ligand to which morphine molecules bind, the tiny receptor on the surface of some cells within the brain and body that receives the pain-killer's chemical message the way a modem receives only computer code. Her discovery sent a wave of excitement through the scientific commu-nity. A group of Scottish neuroscientists were particularly intrigued. *Why would God put a narcotic receptor in the human brain?* they wondered. And then they set out to verify the answer their logic suggested: Perhaps the brain has its own opium-like messengers! They discovered that it did indeed, and they identified the chemicals we now know as endorphin and enkephalin. This discovery, built on the foundation Pert laid, shed light on how the body's natural pain-killing and pleasure-giving capacity operates.

Since her initial discovery of the opiate ligand, Candace Pert has been tracking related findings. One fascinating body of work has been the discovery of groupings of cells showing a high concentration of opiate receptors in various locations throughout the brain and body. One such location is the dorsal horn on the back side of the spinal cord, which is the area within the nervous system where all input regarding bodily sensations first comes together to be processed. "In fact," Pert says, "we have found that in virtually all locations where information from any of the five senses . . . enters the nervous system, we will find a high concentration of neuropeptide receptors" (*Molecules of Emotion*, 142). Because pleasure receptors abound where sensory input is processed, we can take great pleasure in the simple processes of seeing, hearing, tasting, smelling, and touching.

Opportunities to enjoy visual input abound. Looking out from a scenic overlook is a pleasure, as is something as simple as gazing from our kitchen window at a familiar backyard. Sometimes the everyday combinations of sun and clouds and blue sky strike us as gorgeous and breathtaking.

We enjoy scents in a similar way. We pick up the heart-warming scent of lilacs from across the street as we walk by. As we sit in a late morning meeting, the aroma from the cafeteria where lunch is being prepared finds its way to us and helps us anticipate our upcoming meal. A sense of longing is stirred again when we smell the perfume or cologne of our beloved, and we may sniff the letters they send for a hint of their scent. We can remember for a lifetime the smells of Grandma and Grandpa's house, and we savor the warm feelings we used to get there whenever we smell Old

Spice (Grandpa's aftershave), baking bread (Grandma's specialty), or even the odor that reminds us of their musty basement.

Consider next our enjoyment of taste. We can take pleasure in the sweetness of the honey we drizzle onto our morning cereal, the tart burst of red pomegranate seeds, or the salty crunch of roasted almonds. Through an incomprehensibly complex system, the current state of the cells and fluids in our bodies is constantly being assessed. Evaluation becomes feedback as information regarding the balance and needs of the system is translated into a language we can comprehend: craving. We hunger and thirst for just the right combination. We open up the refrigerator and in an instant reach for the drink or the snack that ends up "hitting the spot." We walk down the aisle at the grocery store and in moments are able to pick out those items containing the nutrients our bodies need. Then, as we take these substances in, our sense of taste tells us we got it right and are reaching the goals our bodies have set for us.

Although the receptors for most of our senses reside in our heads, enjoyment is not an experience that happens only from the neck up. Music makes the hair cells within the cochlea of the inner ear tremble, and these receptors pass their message along the auditory nerve to the auditory cortex of the brain, just centimeters from the ear itself. But our listening pleasure only begins as auditory stimulation. Natural, opium-like chemicals bind with receptors throughout our bodies. This, the body's "pleasure system," is recruited and stirred into activity by the sounds and melodies that "move" us.

As he listened over and over again to the description of the "high" experienced by drug addicts, it occurred to veteran addiction researcher Avram Goldstein that he had heard these kinds of "chills" and "thrills" described before—by his friends who didn't use drugs. They were audiophiles describing their response to great music. So he set up an ingenious experiment: He gave a group of music lovers a dose of naloxone, a drug that temporarily clogs the opiate receptors in the brain and body and keeps heroin addicts from getting high. Then he had them listen to their favorite arias and rate the experience. Goldstein's hunch was verified: Their emotional and bodily responses to the music were blunted. They were much less likely to get goosebumps or to be moved to tears at the points in the score they usually found most ecstatic. Apparently, when we enjoy pleasing patterns of sensory stimulation, the body's pleasure system responds in a way that is similar to, although certainly less intense than, the responses of drug addicts enjoying their crude pleasure ("Thrills in Response to Music," 126–29).

Willard Gaylin offers this descriptive account of the thrill we can experience listening to music: "There are certain notes and combinations of notes that have nothing to do with intellect, rationality, ideation and that inevitably cause a kind of chill to be felt across the back of my neck and give me almost a literal feeling of being lifted out of my seat" (*Feelings*, 198). Gaylin wrote this description some twenty years ago, but the more recent work of some curious and creative researchers reminded me of it. They put a Mozart tape in a portable stereo and set it next to a cage of baby chicks. They watched as these tiny animals shuddered at the precise moments in the score that we humans also find most moving! Apparently, our ability to take pleasure in sound comes quite naturally.

Full-bodied enjoyment also occurs when we enjoy tactile stimulation—as we sink into a warm tub or feel the caress of a loving hand, for example. One of my favorite memories is a tactile one: rubbing the palms of my hands across the bumpy green carpet in the living room of my Aunt Ida and Uncle Hubert's home. Considering how good it feels to have our bodies touched, stroked, and rubbed, it is not surprising that massage has been found to stimulate the production of dopamine, the primary chemical messenger within the pleasure circuitry of the brain (Field, "Massage Therapy Effects," 1270–81).

Because the rich and varied input from our senses so often remains at the edges of our awareness, it is impossible to recognize by simply considering the matter just how much each one adds to our enjoyment of life. We are so accustomed to sensory stimulation that we take it for granted. However, we can begin to develop such an appreciation by considering the lives of people who have lost one of their senses or even a portion of their previous sensory range. Their sense of loss can be quite poignant, enough to remind those of us who retain a full repertoire to stop and more fully access the depth of enjoyment that remains available to us.

Helen Keller wrote that "people dependent upon their eyes and ears seldom understand the wealth of life that is tangible" ("The World Through Three Senses," 223). In addition to encouraging a greater awareness of touch, she also pointed out that most men don't even know the color of their wives' eyes—even though she could not see, she challenged those of us who can to enjoy that sense more completely.

One man who developed anosmia—the medical term for the loss of smell—described how distraught he was, and how the magnitude of the loss caught him off guard: "Sense of smell? I never gave it a thought. You don't normally give it a thought. But when I lost it—it was like being struck blind. Life lost a good deal of its savour—one doesn't realise how much 'savour' is smell. You *smell* people, you *smell* books, you *smell* the city, you *smell* the spring—maybe not consciously, but as a rich unconscious background to everything else. My whole world was suddenly radically poorer" (Sacks, *The Man Who Mistook His Wife for a Hat*, 159).

"It is almost as if we have forgotten how to breathe," said another anosmic woman. "I feel empty, in a sort of limbo," echoed a third patient, who found that without his sense of smell he was unable to enjoy meals (Ackerman, *A Natural History of the Senses*, 41). Those of us who take smell for granted are surprised to learn that many anosmics become quite depressed, some inconsolable for a time, and a few even commit suicide (Douek, "Olfaction and Medicine," viii).

It doesn't surprise us that someone who goes blind might feel bereft.

51

But I read an interesting case study that did surprise me. Neurologist Oliver Sacks describes the case of Mr. I., a painter who went colorblind after a brain injury he suffered in a car accident. He could still see, but saw in black and white only. Following the accident, Mr. I. could still look at all the colors on his favorite paintings and match them exactly to his standardized color chart from memory, but he could no longer see colors or access the sense of a color in his mind's eye.

> "You might think," Mr. I. said, "loss of color vision, what's the big deal? Some of my friends said this, my wife sometimes thought this, but to me, at least, it was awful, disgusting."
>
> Mr. I. could hardly bear the changed appearances of people ("like animated grey statues") any more than he could bear his own appearance in the mirror: he shunned social intercourse and found sexual intercourse impossible. He saw people's flesh, his wife's flesh, his own flesh, as an abhorrent grey; "flesh-colored" now appeared "rat-colored" to him. . . .
>
> He found foods disgusting due to their greyish, dead appearance and turned increasingly to black and white foods . . . olives . . . rice . . . coffee and yogurt. . . . His own brown dog looked so strange to him now that he even considered getting a Dalmatian. . . .
>
> He was depressed once by a rainbow, which he saw only as a colorless semicircle in the sky. . . .
>
> The first weeks of his achromatopsia were thus weeks of an almost suicidal depression. (An Anthropologist on Mars, 6–7)

On the "Touch" video from the Nova series The Mystery of the Senses, a woman who lost both legs at the knee in an accident describes how her dreams have taken on a reminiscent quality. "I'm walking in the sand and I can feel the sand going through my toes and I can feel the ocean water on my feet and the cold. Or I can feel myself running and having the muscles contracting all through my legs." Her grief over her loss becomes apparent as she continues her description, her voice trembling with emotion: "But it's a dream and I wake up, and I feel like, *Wow, where are they? They're supposed to be there.*"

Most patients never recover lost sensory abilities. However, when we consider the experience of a few who have, it is interesting to contrast the depth of sorrow over their initial loss with the sometimes giddy relishing of the sense following its restoration. The 11 March 1998 *Hindustan Times* shared the case of a gifted painter whose hearing was restored after decades of deafness. Within days of his operation he was up and painting again, but he spent most of his time "identifying sounds and distinguishing one from the other." His immense enjoyment of the simple sensory experiences that he had been living without was summed up by the reporter: "With each passing day it seems as if Gujral has been transported to a totally new world with far greater possibilities." Likewise, an anosmic woman who was cured through a combination of surgery and steroid treatment likened the recovery of her sense of smell to "making love again after a long interval" (Douek, "Olfaction and Medicine," xix).

The joy people describe as they recover capacities that the rest of us take for granted provides a great reminder. What better time than now to take the cue from an anosmic patient described by Ingelore Ebberfeld, who exclaimed, "If my sense of smell recovered, I would take a year off [to enjoy it]!" We can't afford a year, but wouldn't it be a good idea to spend a day—or at least a few minutes now and then—more fully enjoying the sensory input that remains available to us?

Take a walk and absorb yourself in the visual beauty that surrounds you. The kaleidoscope of colors and shapes all about us can capture our interest if we allow them to, if we will release our mental images and disengage from our internal dialogue for a time. Even on a cold and gray day, subtle contrasts will emerge in bold relief against the seemingly dead winter landscape once you have quieted your thoughts and begun attending to what is there. Practice observing sounds in a similar way: Pause from your usual rush and just passively attend. Simply notice how the world around you registers auditorily.

We can enjoy even the tastes that usually seem bland to us—if we just take the time to attend carefully. The chewy granules in a slice of plain wheat bread and the natural sweetness of a glass of milk provide us with opportunities for appreciation that are readily accessible.

Exercises in touch can be the most rewarding. Take some time to give a loved one a back rub, varying the pressure and pace of your touch. Have the person return the favor while you enjoy the variations in tactile stimulation. Enjoy the textures of different clothing items or try rubbing an assortment of textured materials against your skin.

There is no need for an exhaustive list cataloguing all possible activities. The key is to get started in one or two small ways. Then, your own intuition and creativity will guide you in directions that are the most productive and enjoyable for you. Eventually, instead of an exercise, enjoying your senses will become a way of life.

Reclaiming the Joy of Movement

You are not a tree condemned to a small plot while the wind and world abuses you. You can stretch and run and dance and work.
—Og Mandino

You are playing tag with a two-year-old nephew. His movements are not well coordinated, but he stumbles after you the best he can. To maintain his balance, he flails his arms about as he runs. He is giggling uncontrollably. Drool begins running down his jaw, and his eyes are welling up. These are tears of joy. You tag him and then take two big steps across the lawn. He is trying to keep up, but he's running out of steam, stumbling even more, once or twice even falling to the ground. It won't be long now. Like a matador, you wait until he is about to reach you and then quickly move to one side. Surprised by your move, he loses it. A final fit of laughter does him in. He collapses on the grass in an exhausted, satisfied heap. You flop down beside him and catch the gleam in his eye. What a way to spend a few minutes on a spring afternoon!

One reason we fail to enjoy our bodies as much as we could is that we tend to view them as static things, entities to be judged "good" or "bad" in any given slice of time. However, our bodies are not frozen statues to be sculpted to our liking. They are marvelously dynamic instruments designed to move and breathe and respond to life in an endless series of moments, instruments that tire as energy is expended and then miraculously recover their vitality with rest.

Our kinesthetic and proprioceptive systems comprise what has been called by some our sixth sense, which processes the position of our limbs and the movement of our bodies through space. We enjoy dancing, skiing, and taking a walk in part because of the pleasure inherent in moving our bodies, adjusting our balance, and changing positions. The fact that movement can produce a full-bodied joy experience is never more apparent than when we watch children play. They mimic the flight of birds and the swimming of fish. They run to run, they jump to jump, they twirl to twirl. When we demand that they sit still, they will fidget to fidget!

Only with practice, as we are socialized, do we gradually learn to inhibit our body movements. When it's bedtime, at a restaurant, or at school, it's not okay to move around all we would like to. Learning to control our movements is a necessary and helpful skill that must come early in our self-control repertoire. If we can't sit still, we'll have a hard time paying attention or successfully completing any other task. However, put children in a situation where they are free to move, and move they will!

I remember watching from our front yard a group of young children playing in the cul-de-sac where we lived. They had formed a line and a whole string of them were "following the leader" as they ran from yard to yard. Three-year-old Aaron looked down to watch his legs work. As the group turned to run a different direction, he was so fascinated with his amazing limbs moving to their synchronized beat that he kept traveling along his original trajectory. He varied his speed and took bigger, then smaller steps. He varied his rhythm and almost began skipping. It was clear to me that he was enjoying his body and this one aspect of its vast and wonderful potential for movement.

In our family, we have a tradition that has taken on a life of its own. Jenny and I started it at some point, but it has taken firm root because our kids enjoy it so much and demand almost daily that it continue. Just about every night before bedtime, we have dancing time, pillow time, wrestle time, or soccer time. Once in a while we take a trip to the swimming pool. Pillow time is a giant battle with a half a dozen old pillows that we've collected. Ryan launches them and takes hits from across the room; Aaron prefers hand-to-hand combat. Alex just loves the excitement even though he's not sure what he's supposed to do. He runs up to me, I hold up a pillow, he bounces off it and retreats to take in the intensity of it all, sometimes collapsing to the floor in a fit of laughter. Wrestle time, soccer time, and dancing time are exactly what they sound like. I like wrestle time and dancing time somewhat less because without the pillows or balls I'm the only prop, so my body has to keep all three of the kids busy. Apparently, however, being lifted up into the air by the feet, rolled over on the ground, guided through dance movements, given full-body hugs, and generally mauled in a variety of other ways is a pleasurable experience, because at times they aren't satisfied with the pillows or soccer and demand wrestling or dancing.

After the kids have tried out an activity of this sort once, they typically won't forget it or allow us to drop it from our repertoire. Alex, who is only two years old, already expresses a preference for different activities on different days. It's not unusual for him to walk up to me in the evening and with a pleading look on his face tug at my leg and say, "Dan-sing Ta-eem!" Fortunately, he can usually be pacified with one of the other activities even after he has put in a request. However, Jenny and I have noticed that if we try to put the kids to bed without first having done at least *something* physical, they seem to be more irritable and restless and have a more difficult time winding down for sleep. (Of course, if we do any of these activities too close to bedtime, they have an even harder time settling down.)

Since I'm typically tired at the end of the day, I must admit that sometimes these activities seem burdensome. At least they did until I had an experience that taught me how fulfilling they have been for me as well. I had been away from home for a couple of days at a professional conference in La Jolla, California. One of the presenters walked us through a visualization exercise. He directed us to think of a time when things had felt complete in our lives, when we felt content and connected with others in a satisfying way. A time when things seemed right between us and the world. A time when we were "vibrantly, passionately alive," as he put it. As I sat with my eyes closed, I probed my life for experiences that fit his description. I thought of peaceful times spent enjoying the beauties of nature. I thought of moments of professional achievement. Time spent with friends or family certainly fit what he was describing. But then a multisensory image flooded my consciousness. In my mind's eye, ear, and body, I was downstairs with the boys chucking pillows! It felt so good to sense the energy in that room, to watch the excitement and joy on their faces, to see them moving about, to feel my arm draw back to launch a pillow. These activities that I thought were for my children have become one of the highlights of my life as well!

Unfortunately, today we have more ways to avoid movement than to engage in it. If we watch enough movement on our television sets, our brains seem to tell us we have had enough, even though our bodies cry out, thirsting for some of their own. "Our machines are disturbingly lively," Donna Haraway writes, "and we ourselves frighteningly inert." I thought about Haraway's words recently when we were talking with some friends who had just seen digital TV for the first time. "The screen looked more like a window," they said, "like you could have reached in and touched whatever was on screen." When I hear comments about TV being "almost real," I wonder where we are headed. Will we someday say, "That real experience was so great—almost as good as TV"?

We Americans have cars that do most of our moving for us. A pair of Yugoslavian visitors spent some time with our family a couple of years ago. We asked them what the biggest difference was between life in America and life in their country. "Here you drive almost everywhere," they said. "You even drive out to the mailbox to get your mail!" (They had that one wrong—I would simply stop at the mailbox on my way into the driveway so that I wouldn't have to walk out there later.) By contrast, our guests walked or rode bicycles almost everywhere.

Not only do we avoid movement, we deodorize our bodies to minimize the olfactory evidence that they have been moving. With all of our modern conveniences, unless we are careful we could spend much of our lives sitting still. Before we do, let's remember that the younger members of our species sit still only when it's forced upon them, and even then not very well. We ought to follow their lead and get moving again.

Next time you take a walk, try closing your eyes several times for a few moments at a time while you focus solely on your limbs and their movements. Simply appreciate your muscles and your body and your ability to move about as you choose. Freestyle dancing is another activity that provides an opportunity to experiment with the joy of movement. Try it alone, at least at first, since self-consciousness robs attention from the process of enjoyment. Turn on some music and allow your body to move in response to whatever feelings arise.

10 Enjoying What We Do

If a country is governed wisely . . . people enjoy their food, take pleasure in being with their families, spend weekends working in their gardens, delight in the doings of the neighborhood.
—Tao Te Ching

Do you enjoy what you do?

When someone asks us this question, we usually answer in terms of our work. We may describe what we get out of our work, or evaluate how satisfied we are that we chose our particular vocation. On some days, when we're thinking outside the usual limits, we might describe for the questioner how we spend our leisure time.

Consider for a moment the other things you do. How much do you enjoy them? I'm talking about the things you do no matter where you are, no matter what work you do or where you go on vacation. How much do you enjoy things like . . .

- eating?
- sitting?
- breathing?
- walking?
- resting?
- looking?

When my friend Ken Rodgers was in graduate school, he and a classmate were assigned to lead a group therapy session every Thursday night. They decided to go out to dinner together every week before group. It would give them time to talk over the work they were doing, as well as a rare chance to splurge and enjoy themselves as students on tight incomes.

When they first set up these weekly dinner appointments, Ken's colleague said, "I have to warn you, I really enjoy my food."

"That's okay," Ken responded, "so do I."

Ken didn't think a thing of it again until their first dinner together.

With the first bite of food, his friend closed his eyes and sighed. Then he let out an audible moan as he chewed. "Oh, that's good," he said with an ecstatic smile on his face.

"Throughout that dinner and each one thereafter," Ken told me, "I saw this guy enjoy food in a way that I didn't know was possible—or perhaps had forgotten."

I laughed when Ken first told me this story, and just about everyone I have passed it on to since has responded by laughing. It strikes us as funny, even odd, that someone would enjoy himself so thoroughly.

We want to experience happiness—both as an outcome and in the process of living—and most of our other pursuits are simply the routes by which we hope to arrive at that blessed state. That may sound ridiculously self-evident. Why, then, do we so often forget about enjoying the process and instead lock our sights exclusively on the outcome we are striving for? We end up taking the pursuits quite seriously and treating enjoyment itself as a luxury, as a trivial matter, or as something to be ignored altogether. By way of contrast, George Leigh Mallory, the daring British mountaineer, did not forget the process. Enjoyment was never a trivial matter to him, as demonstrated by his own words:

> The first question which you will ask and which I must try to answer is this, "What is the use of climbing Mount Everest?" and my answer must at once be, "It is no use." There is not the slightest prospect of any gain whatsoever. Oh, we may learn a little about the behavior of the human body at high altitudes, and possibly medical men may turn our observation to some account for the purposes of aviation. But otherwise nothing will come of it. We shall not bring back a single bit of gold or silver, not a gem, nor any coal or iron. We shall not find a single foot of earth that can be planted with crops to raise food. It's no use. So, if you cannot understand that there is something in man which responds to the challenge of this mountain and goes out to meet

it, that the struggle is the struggle of life itself upward and forever upward, then you won't see why we go. What we get from this adventure is just sheer joy. And joy is, after all, the end of life. We do not live to eat and make money. We eat and make money to be able to enjoy life. That is what life means and what life is for.

Did Mallory live to climb? No, he lived and climbed that he might enjoy!

I am always given cause to rethink how seriously I am taking my commitment to enjoy life when I visit my friend Tim. Tim has a fatal degenerative disease called Huntington's Chorea. As his body has deteriorated, he has gradually lost most of his physical abilities. In fact, he can now no longer dress himself and must wear a diaper because he has lost bowel and bladder control. Speaking is a labor. He has been gradually losing his coordination for a long time, and has recently begun having trouble walking without help. Tim is also losing his physical attractiveness. As his disease has progressed, he has lost his hair in patches, has developed open sores on his skin, cuts himself quite frequently, and can no longer groom himself.

Combine his body's appearance with its awkwardness and growing incompetence, and from our culture's perspective, Tim would never be described as having a "great body." Fortunately for him, that is not the perspective he has been taking. Although he suffers profound bodily limitations, the enjoyment that comes through the body is not lost on him. Although he has a hard time raising the food to his mouth, Tim enjoys the food he eats at each meal. Spaghetti with French bread is his favorite, and more than once I have seen the remains of such meals on his face and clothes.

Every time I visit Tim, he wants to go out for a walk. When we do, as we walk out the front door of his nursing home, without fail he struggles to produce the words, "It's *nice* out here." Unlike most of us, "nice" for

Tim could mean sunshine or rain or even snow or sleet. He used to live in Boston, and when the winter weather is the worst, he claims to feel the most at home. Tim will not allow the weather to deter him. He loves to be out in the world, enjoying the trees, the sky, the sights, sounds, and smells. He also loves the feel of the world and occasionally lies down on the grass on the spur of the moment and relishes the experience.

In spite of what is missing for Tim, you could never convince him that he doesn't have a great body. And you couldn't convince me either. Even with all he has lost, he remains able to enjoy as much of life as he *can* experience. And he seems to cherish it all the more. From Tim's perspective, those of us who complain about our bodies because we don't like the exact proportion of our nose or thighs must be like a driver complaining about her Rolls Royce because she doesn't care for the color of the trim.

We should take a lesson from Tim. We have *great* bodies. We should never again let anyone—including ourselves—talk us out of thinking so. For isn't it how thoroughly we enjoy what we do with them, and not so much how they look or exactly how well they function, that truly means the most?

When was the last time you enjoyed something in the way my friend Ken's colleague enjoyed his food? Perhaps an even more important question is, when will the next time be? When will you next take the kind of pleasure in a simple walk that my friend Tim takes, appreciating the weather, the green grass, and whatever else you happen to notice along your way? It is not all that difficult to do. We just have to put aside the other thoughts and concerns that could distract us and immerse ourselves in the pleasure of what we are doing here and now.

11

Becoming Independent of Raw Material

He who knows that enough is enough will always have enough.
—Lao-tzu

Perhaps the most meaningful differences between people can be found in their varying levels of enjoyment. In this regard, there are undeniable gaps. Some seem able to lead lives of happiness and fulfillment, while others drudge on in boredom, meaninglessness, and misery. We have been exploring the possibility that the true difference between the "haves" and the "have-nots" in this regard is not to be found in any of the places we have always looked for it. The key gap is not financial prosperity, social influence, athletic prowess, or physical attractiveness. Once we recognize that enjoyment does not flow from the outcomes we so often pursue, we will no longer be so surprised when we see rich people who are miserable, or gifted athletes or entertainers who are addicted to drugs.

The fact is, a child in El Salvador is born with the same built-in capacity to enjoy his meals as a child in New Hampshire has, even though one of those children's meals might consist simply of rice and beans and a small range of fruits and vegetables. Whether either of those children will appreciate their food as adults depends less on the menu options available to them than on how well they have developed their capacity for enjoyment, how sensitive they are to the tastes they do experience, how pleased they are by the stimulation that is available to them.

Amazingly enough, this is one aspect of life in which the playing field remains relatively level, regardless of where we live, what kind of work we do, and what our standing may be socially or monetarily. That's great news for those of us seeking to enhance our enjoyment of life: It can be done without getting a new job or a nose job.

I've noticed in my own life that it is not necessarily the quality of the music I'm listening to that inspires me. My own capacity to be inspired depends more on the spirit I'm in as I listen. I now understand that it's not the view itself that brings ecstasy, because in a certain frame of mind I can be delighted by the plainest of scenes. Most surprising to me: I've discovered that my reward depends not on the company I keep but on the eyes through which I see them. (I am happy to report that I have been enjoying other people a lot more since learning this.)

To me, the most compelling evidence that enjoyment does not spring from the raw material available in our lives comes from studying the life of Helen Keller. By most standards, here was a woman who had every reason to be a miserable person. She was missing the two senses the rest of us rely on the most. However, she did not respond to her situation by becoming bitter and resentful. As one of her friends once expressed it: "The fact that a person is deaf and blind makes people almost shudder if they take time to think about it. And then they go into a meeting and there she is, smiling and radiant. Certainly not talking very well, in a way that was very easy to understand, but what she said was happy, it was a message of hope. People might say, Gee, I wish I had as happy an outlook on life as this woman" (Freudberg, "An Optimist in Spite of All," audiocassette, side A).

Is it really possible that someone would envy Helen Keller? That idea struck me as absurd when I first heard the above quote on a National Public Radio program about her life. However, it also sparked my interest, and I began reading her autobiographical works. Then I started to envy her myself. She loved life. She could thoroughly enjoy the sunshine on her face, the smell of a child's skin, the softness of a dog's hair. I consider myself blessed: Instead of just envying her, I also began learning from her, and I will pass along some more of the lessons from her life in later chapters.

Please consider a final piece of evidence that enjoyment is up to us, that we are not dependent on the raw material of our lives to provide it. Consider the life of my favorite TV weatherman. For years I have admired the work of Mark Eubank, and I have been engaged in a sort of case study of him from afar. He is the meteorologist for KSL, the NBC affiliate in Salt Lake City, and no one gets more excited about the weather—or much else, for that matter—than he does. Whenever I watch the evening news broadcast, I am impressed that he has found something else intriguing to report. Just how much can you do with a weather report? He has proven that you can do quite a bit. Using props or graphics, he demonstrates how a temperature inversion or a cold front works, or he relates some current weather event to some obscure fact from the history of Utah's weather. He has even written a book about Utah weather!

The weather. A topic so often paired with boredom it has become cliché. ("How dull was the conversation? We had nothing to talk about but the weather!") And yet here is someone to whom the weather is a source of fascination. He has found it interesting enough to make a career of it. Not only that, but he gives the rest of us a taste of what we are missing when we take the weather for granted.

Mark Eubank is an ideal example of the enjoyable life. His passion and enthusiasm constitute undeniable evidence that our level of pleasure is not determined by the quality or intensity of stimulation in our lives. Enjoyment does not emanate from a rare source; it is not ignited by only a narrow range of activities. A weatherman with a full, rich life proves that enjoyment does not spring from the raw material of our lives but from the way we approach that material.

I invite you to take a step back and consider your own life. Have you perhaps locked your sights on the wrong target? Are you caught up in the single-minded pursuit of some kind of raw material—any kind? Have you convinced yourself that happiness will flow from what you achieve, once you finally achieve it?

If you have been on this path, you are not alone. Many people live and die without ever realizing that their life's road was a detour that consumed much of their journey. To borrow a metaphor from bestselling author Stephen Covey, they work their tails off climbing the ladder of success, never discovering that it is leaning against the wrong wall. If this discussion hits home, please read on: I'm convinced that you'll want to get off the detour once you've explored a more direct route, that you'll gladly move your ladder once you've found a more productive wall to climb.

12

Recovering from Too Much

I lost touch. I lost such touch.
—Arnold Weinstein

At a professional conference, I once heard Gordon Foote, a psychotherapist from Flower Mound, Texas, tell of a patient who was working to give up pornography, masturbation, and his occasional hiring of prostitutes. One day this client's wife came to Foote's office, seeking advice. "What do you think of these?" she asked, cupping her hands under her breasts. Caught off guard by her question, the only response he could think of was, "You must have a very good reason for asking that." As it turned out, her husband was trying to convince her to undergo breast augmentation surgery. Following a protracted period of overstimulation, he was making an effort to turn away from all of that intensity and to focus his affections solely upon a single, real woman. As he did, he found her wanting: Her breasts were not large or shapely enough. Who knows what else he would have changed about her if he could have.

Foote's message to this woman was critical, and it is the point I make to anyone who is trying to exit the cycle of addiction: The problem is not in the quality of the stimulation available in normal, everyday life, but in your current sensitivity to it. That husband could come to enjoy his wife and in time perhaps even be thrilled by her as he was hoping to be. But the kind of changes he was trying to get her to make were not the changes that really needed to be made. What needed augmentation was his sensitivity, not her breasts, and that would take time and patience, working and waiting on his part.

Imagine that you were cold, and that you became impatient and dissatisfied with the amount of warm air that was being pumped out by your furnace. So, instead of patiently waiting for the house to get warmer in its usual, natural way, you decided to build a fire in the living room. Well, as the fire heated up, the thermostat would get the message that the room was warm enough, and the furnace would produce even less warm air. In response, you might decide to stoke the fire in the living room in an attempt to heat up the place some more. The problem is, the living room is the only one in the house that's warm—but even so, not consistently warm. Instead, it cycles between being too hot for a time and then back to too cold.

Just as the furnace shuts down in response to feedback, the production and activity of the body's natural pleasure chemicals tend to shut down any time an individual subjects himself or herself to artificially intense stimulation. Continuing our furnace metaphor: If you want to return your house to a point where it is more consistently and evenly heated, you have to get the furnace to kick on again. To do so, you will have to put out the fire completely and wait patiently for the thermostat to register the correct temperature. Then the furnace will get the message that it's needed again, and its production of warm air will be restored. Before an addict's satisfaction with normal life can increase, he or she has to tolerate dissatisfaction for a time.

The recovery of our capacity for enjoyment does not occur as quickly as a furnace "kicking on" again. It depends on the interplay of organic processes as well as on psychological and spiritual components, each of which has a pace and timing all its own. The organic processes in particular are not reactive to every minuscule, day-to-day alteration but tend to hold in a stable way at a given level. This is one of the great miracles of the human body: It is responsive without being so reactive that our lives become chaotic and unpredictable. Nonetheless, over time the body's production of the "ahh" and "ah-hah" chemicals does increase, and the brain's pleasure centers become more responsive, helping to gradually restore our capacity for enjoyment.

There are many natural processes that adjust this way when they receive feedback about the intensity of stimulation. When we first walk into a building after being outside on a sunny day, our vision may "black out" for a split second and leave us unable to see anything at all. Our eyes quickly adjust to the new environment, adapting their sensitivity to the decreased level of light.

If you and I were to sit quietly together for an hour in a soundproof room, initially we would hear nothing but the silence, so accustomed are we to being bombarded by a high level of noise every day. However, over time we would discover that there are things to be heard in our quiet little room. Each other's breathing, for example, and eventually, if we attend carefully, perhaps even the soft blinking of each other's eyes!

Our awareness of these soft sounds takes longer to recover than did our vision after we came in from the sunlight. Restoring sensitivity of other kinds can take even longer. Some patients with heart disease or other illnesses are prescribed a low-salt diet by their physicians. To people who are used to pouring salt on their food before they even taste to see if it's needed, the reduction in taste intensity that comes with this change can be a real challenge. However, if they stick with their new "bland" diet, after a few weeks they begin to report some surprises. "You know, corn has a taste all its own that I've been drowning out with so much salt." The flavor may not be as rich or as full, but its subtleties and nuances can be enjoyed more and more over time.

The brain's pleasure centers themselves and the chemicals by which they send their messages can recover from desensitization, although the process may be even more drawn out than any of the others we have discussed so far. For this reason, one of the most difficult stages of recovery from a serious addiction is the period of abstinence following a period of intense involvement with the substance or behavior. As one client of mine described how flat and difficult life was during that period, I realized that his body must be almost completely devoid of the brain and body chemicals that bring enjoyment and pleasure. His system had become accustomed to frequent deluges of heroin and hence had shut down its own production of natural opiate substances, endorphin and enkephalin. In the midst of his most intense abuse of the drug, he stayed with it not only because the drug brought him pleasure but because nothing else in his life could anymore! He had stopped caring about what he ate; everything tasted bland to him, and food had lost its capacity to make him feel satisfied. He had stopped taking walks by the river near his apartment because the aesthetic pleasures he had once enjoyed were now empty for him.

My friend's first few weeks without drugs were the most difficult because he had to go back to a life of more subdued stimulation even though it brought him little pleasure at the time. His typical breakfast had been "a Big Slam of Mountain Dew and a box of jelly doughnuts." Wheat toast and fruit juice seemed so bland he could hardly stand it. However, I cheered him on and assured him that he was on the right track. He came to believe that someday, now that he had left the cacophony behind him, whispers would become audible again.

Several weeks into his treatment, I remember walking outside with him one evening during the break from our nightly group session. The rush of fresh, cool air as we exited the building and the sight of pastel-colored clouds along the western horizon were so refreshing after ninety minutes of therapy, I let out an "Ahhh!" of pleasure. He said, as though he were enjoying something that subtle for the first time in a long time, "That is nice."

We may not be coming down off of heroin, but our lives are overflowing with stimulation. As we reduce the intensity, we will have to tolerate periods of flatness and boredom, just as my friend did. It will be tempting to go back to our usual patterns of stimulation and consumption to fill the gaps. We must retain hope that these periods of seeming silence are actually filled with symphonies we can no longer hear because our ears have been deadened. If we are patient and persistent, we will begin to see that moments of seeming emptiness can actually be full enough to be enjoyed.

13

Discovering Hunger's Hidden Treasures

Let us remain as empty as possible so that God can fill us up.
—Mother Teresa

I have mentioned that my family didn't own a TV set when I was a kid. That's not to say that I didn't enjoy watching TV. One night early in December when I was still in grade school, we went down to Greg and Darin Gibby's house to watch the Christmas specials. What a treat that was! We were fascinated by the stories of the Grinch and Frosty the Snowman. Sometimes my mom let me go over to Steve Rich's house after school, and Steve and I would watch *Daniel Boone* or *Star Trek*.

With regard to TV, I must have seemed like the dentist's daughter whose parents don't let her eat sweets at home, who comes to a birthday party with the cake and ice cream and party favors and thinks she's in heaven. I think back on my delight at the time with what little TV I did view, and it contrasts sharply with the boredom of some of the junior couch potatoes I've observed. This observation hints that hunger might contain some hidden treasures, that by offering us less, my parents may have actually provided us with more.

Research has verified what I experienced firsthand. Put yourself in the place of the subjects who participated in the following study: You show up at the lab for seven days straight. Once there, you spend a half hour eating ice cream and listening to music. Then, after each session, you rate how much you enjoyed the experience that day. Doesn't sound like a bad way to earn some extra credit for a college class, does it? The study I have just described was conducted by researchers Danie Kahneman and Jackie Snell. They found that, as the week wore on, instead of continuing to find the experience as satisfying as it was when they first tried it, participants' enjoyment dwindled over time.

Kahneman and Snell had another group undergo a different experience. They listened to music too, but instead of ice cream they ate plain, low-fat yogurt for the seven days. Their taste for the yogurt actually increased instead of decreasing as the days went by. They experienced the exact opposite effect of the growing dissatisfaction described by the ice-cream eaters. Apparently, not only can less be more, it can become even more over time!

Given the appeal of the intensity trap and its powerful hold once we are in its grasp, we are fortunate that there is also a more fruitful path, a sequence I call "the cycle of enjoyment" (see top half of figure on p. 24). It is a process that mirrors the cycle of addiction in many ways. One's sensitivity, tolerance of deprivation, and satisfaction with life all change with each turn through the sequence, only in this case they increase. Thus our capacity for enjoyment can expand instead of shrinking over time.

Lasting enjoyment is like a crop that must be sown and nurtured before it can be harvested. Working and waiting are indispensable elements of enjoyment's most successful pursuits, demanding of us discipline, patience, sacrifice, and effort. When we find ourselves in a state of wanting, we don't have to try to satisfy it or run from it. There exists also the difficult but rewarding option of tolerating our wants and desires by settling into and coming to terms with them. This approach exercises and expands our true power, for when we refuse to be bullied by desire but instead respond to it as we choose, we are in control of our lives. Once we are willing to pursue enjoyment patiently and in a disciplined manner, even to the point of tolerating deprivation, an entirely new world opens up to our view. More accurately, we have an entirely new view of the same old world. We need do no more than look, listen, taste, smell, touch, and move, because we do each of these with new eyes, ears, tongues, noses, hands, and bodies.

I love the way M. Scott Peck describes the payoff of working and waiting while accepting less for a time: "Delaying gratification is a process of scheduling the pain and pleasure of life in such a way as to enhance the pleasure by meeting and experiencing the pain first and getting it over with. It is the only decent way to live" (*The Road Less Traveled*, 19). By accepting short-term pain—at least if it is pain that has a purpose—we plant the seeds of disproportionate pleasure.

I learned about the paradoxical connection between deprivation and fulfillment from a humble and stately Korean grandmother who was my gracious hostess one afternoon years ago. A colleague and I had been traveling all morning along the hot and dusty roads of the rural Korean village of Kumsan. The literal English translation of *Kumsan* is "Gold Village." The town is known throughout Asia for its fine ginseng, a golden-white root that is now familiar in the West as a nutrition supplement. Early in the afternoon, we arrived at the traditional home of this gentle grandmother. She sat us on the wooden floor of the room that served her family as both living room and bedroom, then disappeared behind delicate paper and wood partitions into the kitchen.

We were relieved to be in from the heat and intrigued by the chopping and whirring and pouring sounds coming from the other room. Before long, she emerged from the kitchen carefully balancing a full platter. She set it before us and motioned for us to eat and drink.

She told us of how her father had grown ginseng, and how her husband and oldest son still worked the same land. She told us of the five-year growing cycle, the shelters that are built to protect each plant, and the other difficulties of growing ginseng. And she spoke with regret about how few people appreciated ginseng as fully as they might if they only experienced its breadth and variety. Then she explained that each of the three treats we were eating from the platter was made from ginseng. There was the warm ginseng tea, which was already familiar to us. But we had never tasted dried ginseng. She described the process of dipping the roots in honey and then spreading them out in the sun to be dehydrated. Ginseng roots are about as long as a carrot and much thicker, so she had chopped them into bite-size pieces when we arrived at her home.

But the highlight of the snack she provided was a sort of "smoothie," ginseng that had been ground to mush and then blended with slushy ice water. We didn't know the Korean word for the drink, so we would later reminisce about the Korean Slurpee. The stately grandmother's delight at our oohs and ahhs was evident, but she humbly shook her head.

"*Shijangi banchan gikali kamshik.*" In English: "Hunger is the best . . ." and then a word I didn't understand. A Korean saying, she explained. I nudged my dictionary from my back pocket and looked up the word *banchan.* English translation: *side dish.* In Korea, the main course for every meal was rice. But it was the rich and spicy side dishes that added flavor to the meal. This was not the best drink we'd ever tasted, she was insisting, we had simply been hot and tired when we had arrived at her home. Our pleasure resulted from the deprivation that had preceded the treat. This was classic Korean modesty, but the message in her axiom rang true nonetheless: No special preparations or exotic spice can flavor a meal quite like hunger can.

What we have considered regarding food is equally true of other kinds of deprivation. Rather than pointless suffering, our times of lacking can become the foundation for enjoyment more exquisite than we could otherwise hope for. Once we have tasted the bitter, we can more fully enjoy the sweet.

Nowhere does the operation of this principle become more apparent than in the life of Helen Keller. She enjoyed her life immensely, in part because her most enjoyable experiences stood out in bold relief against the backdrop of deep wanting.

Helen's description of her experience with Annie Sullivan at the water pump, a most moving human drama, is one of those joyous moments made more meaningful by the scarcity that had preceded it. As her teacher spelled the word W-A-T-E-R again and again into her hand, it finally occurred to Helen that this was language, a lifeline that could breach the void of aloneness that had until then held her captive. Helen realized that she was no longer alone, that she could communicate with another soul. Could greater joy have been possible?

> *It was a wonderful day, never to be forgotten. Thoughts that ran forward and backward came to me quickly—thoughts that seemed to start in my brain and spread all over me. . . . Nothingness was blotted out! I felt joyous, strong, equal to my limitations! Delicious sensations rippled through me, and sweet, strange things that were locked up in my heart began to sing.*
>
> *When the sun of consciousness first shone upon me, behold a miracle! The stalk of my young life that had perished, now steeped in the waters of knowledge, grew again, budded again, was sweet again with the blossoms of childhood. Down in the depths of my being I cried, "It is good to be alive!" I held out two trembling hands to life, and in vain would silence impose dumbness upon me henceforth.*

To me, the most amazing part of Helen's description of that experience is not the relaying of the events themselves, but rather her contention that "That first revelation was worth all those years I had spent in dark, soundless imprisonment. That word 'water' dropped into my mind like the sun in a frozen winter world" (Keller, *Light in My Darkness*, 20–21).

How could Helen say this revelation was worth the suffering that had preceded it when her suffering was so immense? Could this reward really have been out of proportion to its price? Only if it is, as author Neal A. Maxwell claims, that "Some deprivation is an excavation. It is the readying of a reservoir into which a generous God will later pour all that he hath" ("Try the Virtue of the Word of God," audiocassette, side A).

From this perspective, the avoidance of deprivation represents an unwillingness to make room for God. While there is in our culture an almost constant chorus claiming that we need not tolerate deprivation, if we listen closely we can also find messengers singing a different tune.

These voices call for us to leave room so that we do not displace God with the other sources of gratification that can easily fill our lives. Instead of promising more, most of the great spiritual teachers and religious leaders throughout history have extolled the virtues of the simpler, plainer life, of the life we might today see as deprived. Instead of instant payoff and fulfillment, most religions demand sacrifice. Interestingly enough, today many of us are returning to spirituality and religion in search of a fulfillment that the pursuit of our appetites has not provided.

Of the Islamic faith's five pillars of observance, four typically entail some kind of relinquishment. *Siyam* (fasting) is a key method for practicing restraint. During Ramadan faithful Muslims do not eat at all during daylight hours for the entire month. *Zakat* (charity) requires that Muslims give up a percentage of their income and property. *Hajj* (traveling to Mecca) and *Salat* (the five compulsory daily prayers) also require tremendous sacrifice for some. Leading by example, Muhammad himself said, "Poverty is my pride."

Siddhartha Gautama reached enlightenment by following a path of tremendous privation. His early life was characterized by ease and extravagance, but when he ventured beyond that secluded existence, he was confronted with the inevitability of suffering. He turned to a rigorously ascetic life in search of a way to relieve universal suffering. Later he would encourage his followers to pursue a path of balance rather than the extreme austerity he had practiced. Nonetheless, Buddhist practitioners still teach that, because suffering results from desire, we must eliminate desires and the specific goals to which we have become attached in order to reach Nirvana.

I have always been struck by how Jesus responded when people approached him with the intent of becoming disciples and turning their lives over to him. To the scribe who came offering to follow him wherever he went, Jesus warned: "The foxes have holes, and the birds of the air have nests; but the Son of man hath not where to lay his head"

(Matthew 8:19–20). Rather than a full life, he described a life of deprivation. When the ruler who claimed to have kept all of the commandments from his youth asked what he should do to inherit eternal life, Jesus said: "Yet lackest thou one thing: sell all that thou hast, and distribute unto the poor" (Luke 18:18–22). He offered a life that was lacking, at least of material goods. To his disciples, he said, "He that loveth father or mother more than me is not worthy of me: and he that loveth son or daughter more than me is not worthy of me. And he that taketh not his cross, and followeth after me, is not worthy of me" (Matthew 10:37–38).

As these excerpts illustrate, Jesus was constantly warning would-be followers just how much sacrifice the very best life demanded. He was declaring in advance its high price, a bit like the pilot on a commercial airline who announces the flight's destination just prior to departure, lest anyone unknowingly be taken to a place he or she does not intend to go.

We may look at his demand for sacrifice as a sort of test, and certainly it represents that. But Jesus also made it quite clear that there is a deeper value in sacrifice, some inherent benefit in living a life of relative deprivation. In the verse that follows the one just quoted above, he explains, "He that findeth his life shall lose it: and he that loseth his life for my sake shall find it" (Matthew 10:39). Sacrifice, deprivation, and even suffering can actually enhance our lives. Elsewhere, Jesus describes this paradox again:

> And he lifted up his eyes on his disciples, and said, Blessed be ye poor: for yours is the kingdom of God. Blessed are ye that hunger now: for ye shall be filled. Blessed are ye that weep now: for ye shall laugh. . . .
>
> But woe unto you that are rich! for ye have received your consolation. Woe unto you that are full! for ye shall hunger. Woe unto you that laugh now! for ye shall mourn and weep. (Luke 6:20–21; 24–25)

Somehow, Jesus insisted, being poor prepares us for the kingdom of God. Hungering now prepares us to be filled. Weeping now lays the foundation for greater joy in the future. Deprivation, he verifies, can excavate the reservoir into which God can pour.

Throughout the first part of this book we explored how more becomes less; in this chapter we have glimpsed the other side of that coin. Miraculously, less can come to mean so much more to us. If we turn away from the booming voices and flashy images that beckon us to follow appetite's lead, we can still hear the whispers from Muhammad, from Buddha, from Jesus. Our spirit responds to their call for sacrifice just as our appetite responds to an advertiser's promises of more. Although less urgent in its demands, our spirit has a persistent pressing all its own. The question is, which press will we allow to drive us to action? Which promises are we going to believe?

Our society practically force-feeds us instant gratification and indulgence. Nonetheless, if we are willing to forego stimulation, if we deprive ourselves in some helpful ways, we will open ourselves up to a life that is full and rich beyond our current ability to conceive. Brutis Hamilton, former coach of the UCLA men's track team and the 1952 men's Olympic team, observed: "It is one of the strange ironies of this strange life that those who work the hardest, who subject themselves to the strictest discipline, who give up certain pleasurable things in order to achieve a goal, are the happiest men" (Walton, *Beyond Winning*). Amazingly, the reward is always out of proportion to the sacrifice.

To this end, we should all take the opportunity to practice depriving ourselves—not in a perverse sort of way, for the sake of suffering, but for the benefits that such sacrifice can bring to our lives. The following thoughts and practices might be helpful:

1. Fasting

Although going without food can be an exquisitely felt deprivation, when engaged in deliberately as an act of self-discipline or worship it can also be a source of fulfillment. Indeed, going without food can set the table for an emotional and spiritual feast. It is much easier to opt out of this chance to deepen our spirituality and enhance our appreciation, but many who do take it describe it as well worth the sacrifice.

One of the most immediate and obvious payoffs of fasting—appreciation of the food we do have—was noted by fourteen-year-old Alisha Girstein after she observed the Yom Kippur fast for the second time: "When we broke the fast, the first thing I ate was a grape, and it tasted *so* good. It was the sweetest thing."

"The experience of fasting doesn't feel like a deprivation to me," agreed Judith Wieler, "it feels like a gift. To take on a discipline of pushing away the things that confuse or blind or cover the beauty of life. It's kind of like you've got this incredible crystal, but it's covered with dust. And sometimes you have to clean it off" (Freudberg, "Humankind: A Different Sort of Food," audiocassette, program 11).

How strange responses like those can seem to us in the age of addiction, when almost any good news is taken as a reason—perhaps more an excuse—to indulge in even more food than our usual abundance!

2. Opportunities for Silence and Meditation

Many religions provide sanctuaries, places and times where members are free to engage in quiet pondering. When for a time I am denied the chance to talk, the opportunity to hear breaking news about world events, and the control I usually have over the pace at which I complete my daily activities—oh, how good these deprivations are for my soul! These sessions curb my appetites and help calm my frantic seeking for more. And as our need for such serenity grows, today more than ever many people are developing sanctuaries and rituals of their own, independent of organized religion.

3. Depriving Our Kids

One mother pointed out that when she chooses not to give her children everything she can afford to give them, she is "holding back for their sake." Author Fred Gosman points out: "If a telemarketer called and asked to speak to the head of the household, we'd often have to give the phone to the child. . . . They select the movie we rent, select the radio station in the car, choose the restaurant we go to, and the vacation spot" (Gardner, "Advice on Parenting"). He succinctly describes the damage this parenting approach can cause: "Children who always get what they want will want as long as they live" (Gosman, *Spoiled Rotten*, 32).

4. TV-Free Times

I'll stop short of recommending that you throw out your television set, although rich rewards have often been reaped by families who have done so. At least we should have times when TV viewing is prohibited. We may set aside certain times of the day, a day of the week (the Sabbath day for some), or even a TV-free week each year as the Parents Television Council recommends. When the TV is off, our heart rates slow and our consciousness once again becomes self-directed instead of externally driven.

5. Giving Up Some "Necessities"

When our family moved to the small, quiet town of Rexburg, Idaho, we were deprived of some things we had been taking for granted. Our reception of most TV channels was poor. There was no shopping mall in town. Our weekend entertainment options were limited—there were just a couple of movie theaters and a handful of restaurants. What we discovered over time surprised us: The inconvenient life was *wonderful*—quiet, peaceful, serene. Instead of focusing on the news, we were out taking walks and talking with our neighbors. We took frequent rides around town and along country roads in our van. During the summer we took the kids on hikes. In the winter we spent some of our evenings organizing shelves at the local food bank. Since that time, we've tried to maintain a certain level of inconvenience in our lives. We have found that some inconveniences—like riding the bus to the zoo instead of driving, or doing without the evening news—can actually be quite rewarding.

Try taking a longer but more scenic route to get to work or to run errands. The more compulsive you are with regard to speed, the more likely it is that you have prioritized convenience over substance. Chances are, the more difficult this exercise is for you, the more good it will do you, since it will violate that mind-set.

6. *Sexual Moderation*

In his book *Kosher Sex*, Rabbi Shmuley Boteach reminds us that periods of voluntary abstinence from physical intimacy heighten a couple's desire and appreciation for each other. He also points out that such opportunities are often brought on quite naturally by business trips and other brief separations. We can reap the rewards of such experiences, as long as we don't deplete the anticipation that builds during such periods through pornography or fantasizing.

7. *The Sabbath Day*

If we protect it as sacred time, the Sabbath can strengthen our spiritual immune systems against appetite's destructive plague. As Wayne Muller explains:

> *During the Sabbath we disengage from what Abraham Heschel calls "the nervousness and fury of acquisitiveness." We surrender, for a time, our relentless desires. . . . The antidote to craving is rest; we quench our thirst with Sabbath tranquillity. We invite a time in which we can taste what we have been given, take delight in what we already have, and see that it is good. We focus less on our lack, and more on our abundance. As we do, our thirst and hunger for more than we need begins to fall away. In quiet stillness we can identify our genuine needs with more precision, and separate them more easily from our mindless wants and desires. We can feel the difference between happiness—which is often simple and easy, an inner shift toward appreciation and gratefulness for what is before us—and desire, which is often frantic and relentless, cutting the heart with its sharp and painful demands.*
>
> *If we do not disengage, if we stay on the wheel of desire, if*

we do not stop and pray and sing and walk, the pattern of our addictive craving is free to escalate without limit, until we inadvertently create a life with terrible suffering for ourselves and those we love. (Sabbath, 126–27)

Are you permitting your soul to be excavated, prepared as a reservoir into which a generous God can pour all that he has? Even if we don't deliberately set out to deprive ourselves, most of us are missing something for which our heart yearns. We may suffer from an annoying physical ailment, live a schedule that allows us little free time, or be estranged from a relative whose relationship we value. Keep searching if you haven't yet discovered the fruit in these, the sparser areas of your life's garden.

14

Standing Up to Desire

I have learned to seek my happiness by limiting my desires,
rather than in attempting to satisfy them.
—John Stewart Mill

Even if we have seen the potential benefits of deprivation and are convinced that they are worth the price, that won't make the actual experience of being deprived any less difficult or uncomfortable. Even when we undergo deprivation willingly, we typically don't welcome its sidekick: our old acquaintance, desire. Desire is quite powerful and can be quite pushy. However, we don't have to succumb to its control.

My friend Dave Nielson told me about one of the most significant decisions he and his wife, Mercie, ever made. He had completed college and landed a job teaching geography and history at a middle school. They had moved their young family into a modest home in a middle-class neighborhood near the school. Within a year, however, it had become clear that his salary as a teacher could not cover their house payment and living expenses. Should his wife go to work and make other child-care arrangements? Should he get a second job and spend his evenings away from his family? They didn't like either of those options, so they did something very few people are willing to do. They accepted less desirable living conditions. They moved to an older, smaller home.

Dave had just recently retired when he and I talked about that decision. They had been living in their "little green hut," as he affectionately called it, for his entire career. "There were times when we got pretty cramped in that tiny house," he admitted. "At one point, one of my sons even had to sleep on the couch because there wasn't enough room in the bedrooms. My wife has never had much of a kitchen, and that has been hard on her." Looking back, however, he and his family have no regrets. "The kids came home to Mom every day after school. My work allowed me to also be home in the afternoons and off in the summertime, so I was able to spend all of that precious time with the people who matter most to me."

Dave and his family are still reaping the benefits of the sacrifices they made long ago. His kids are decent, happy people, and they all still enjoy the time they spend together as a family. He and his wife are planning for the time when they can move out of their small home, and they will enjoy a new place even more for all the years of sacrifice and anticipation.

Dave and his family have harvested such rich rewards only because at that critical point they had the courage to face their desire for a more comfortable home and say, "Even though you are powerful, you cannot control us." They exercised something far too few of us do: their freedom. They cherished family more than comfort, and they based their choice on that priority. They actively chose their life course instead of allowing themselves to be pushed around by the "need" for more this or more that. The purpose of this chapter is to explore how the rest of us can do what they did—become less dependent on the things we naturally crave and choose to pursue our deepest desires instead.

Our ability to enjoy life depends not only on how we handle what we have but also on how we approach what we *don't* have. When we find ourselves in a state of wanting, we don't have to try to satisfy it or run from it. We can learn to handle this unwanted guest in a way that keeps it from being disruptive in our lives. This approach exercises and expands our true power, for when we refuse to be bullied by desire but instead respond to it as we choose, we establish greater control of our lives. Think for a moment about how different this is from how we usually deal with the state of desire. We typically treat the sense of wanting as something to be indulged on its own terms or banished as quickly as possible. If certain desires have gotten us into trouble in the past, we may even wish that we never experienced them at all.

When one of my clients came in to see me for the first time, it was clear to me that he didn't want to want. During our first meeting, Shane said that he felt his recovery from his addiction was going better than ever: "I've been feeling wonderful lately, and I've only craved alcohol once in the last week." He had recently started a job with a small mail-order company. He had always struggled to stay motivated in his work, but said: "I'm finding that I don't really mind this work. It's not too bad. And it feels good to be productive." He described insecurities that he'd had in the past in his relationship with his girlfriend. "Fortunately," he concluded, "I've hardly felt that at all over the last few weeks. Our relationship is more positive than ever."

When he finished describing how things were going, I had some bad news for Shane: "I know it feels good," I conceded, "but right now your recovery is actually quite fragile. I'll be much more confident you're on the right track when you walk in to a session and say something like: 'I have had some fierce cravings, and they've been a real thorn in my side this week. Work really stinks, I think I probably chose the wrong career, but I'm still showing up and doing my job every day. My girlfriend and I have had several quarrels lately. I get jealous and upset when she describes some of the things that go on at her work because I start worrying about whether I'm good enough for her and whether she'll stay with me. Overall, though, the relationship is positive enough that I'm willing to keep trying to work through the challenges. Even though I'm really frustrated with life right now, I'm determined to stick with it. As hard as life is, it's better than when I was drinking.'"

Shane was mistakenly assuming that his recovery depended on how consistently things in his life went well. His real success would be determined much more by how he handled life when things were not going well. It requires very little character to do the right things when we're feeling good. The most important thing—and the toughest—is to develop the habit of doing the right things even when we don't feel good, sticking to our commitments even when that is the last thing in the world we want to do.

Over time Shane developed a greater ability to tolerate emotional discomfort. He did so in part by developing the ability to see through discomfort's propaganda. He has come to see that how we feel is not the absolute truth about how well our lives are going. The question of whether he is doing what is good for himself and other people has replaced the question of how much suffering he is experiencing as the standard by which he measures his life.

We rob desire of its power when we "face the wreck," when we engage in what John Kabbot-Zinn calls "full-catastrophe living." Instead of running from the void within us that becomes apparent when stimulation ceases, we can make peace with that void. This is a difficult process because most of us don't want to even face the voids in our life, let alone make peace with them. However, as Gary Zukav reminds us, our spiritual growth is not an end run around our agony; rather our agony and despair are our very avenues of growth.

The feeling that something is missing from our lives is, interestingly enough, an accurate assessment. Remember, we are not yet filled with all that God has for us. However, to say that this feeling is accurate is not necessarily to say that it is always a true indication that something needs to—or even can—change immediately. The feeling of "not enough" is as normal as the enjoyment that it supplants at times. Life is, as C. S. Lewis put it, a series of troughs and peaks: "periods of emotional and bodily richness and liveliness . . . alternate with periods of numbness and poverty" (*Screwtape Letters*, 37).

Each one of us feels incomplete because each of us *is* incomplete in some way—indeed, in a variety of ways. We are all flawed and ordinary people. Instead of immediately satisfying our neediness, denying our neediness, or hiding from it behind distracting thoughts and behavior, what if we instead settled into our neediness? What if we were willing to fully experience our desires, cravings, urges, and temptations? What if we were to do nothing in response but tolerate our want, tolerate that feeling of "not enough"? What if we did nothing more than face desire and lean into it?

When desire shows up as an unwanted guest, we typically think we have to pursue one of two options. First, we can accept it—invite it in and then follow where it leads us and do its bidding. Second, we can avoid it—sort of like shutting our blinds and hiding to distract ourselves from its invitations or running out the back door to get away from desire as quickly as we can.

Let's consider a third, more powerful option: We can treat desire in a kind but firm way, as we might any other uninvited and unwanted guest. We can open the door and allow it to come in and sit down—and then politely inform our desire: "You're welcome to stay as long as you'd like, but there were some other things that I was in the middle of, so excuse me while I go about my business."

If you decide to try this approach, you will find that at first desire will not be content to leave you alone. It will chatter away at you, making it hard for you to concentrate or hear other ideas above the racket. You might even find that *you* are not content to leave *desire* alone for long, and catch yourself repeatedly checking to see if it is still there. However, you will also discover that if you hold firm, things will change. Desire does not like to be ignored, and it will eventually take offense and leave you for a time. Not forever, of course; it might return with a vengeance later. However, when it does, you will be better prepared to face it again, knowing that it has less power over you.

It can be quite exhilarating to feel the power of refusing to be bullied by desire. It feels good to face desire and say, "I'm just going to sit with you. Experience you. Get comfortable with you. I'm not going to follow you anymore. I'm not going to run from you anymore. You no longer control my life."

Instead of taking out a home-equity loan in order to build a swimming pool, what if the parents of the kids in the advertisement described earlier provided their kids with nothing more than the time and space to come to terms themselves with their boredom and dissatisfaction? One of my colleagues told me about a series of break-ins and some vandalism that occurred at several cabins near her small town. When the boys responsible for the crimes were caught, one mother called in to a local radio show and defended her son on the air. The underlying problem, she insisted, was that kids like her son had nothing to do. The town was too boring. The city officials responded by building a skate park near the high school.

Don't get me wrong: I like the idea of building parks. However, that mother and those politicians should not expect that the step they have taken will prevent future crime. The excitement of a new attraction may occupy the kids for a time, but sooner or later these kids will have to come to terms with the fact that life is not always exciting. That moment will provide them with the opportunity to choose whether they will once again break the law—or break through their own resistance to working and waiting for greater rewards.

We must not allow boredom to scare us away so easily. On the other side of boredom is a fertile land of ideas and possibilities, a land that can be rich with pleasure. We will arrive there not in spite of but partially because of our willingness to tolerate the desert experience.

Analyzing hieroglyphic poetry from ancient Egypt, Diane Ackerman has concluded that an ever-present yearning for a better life, a desire for self-transformation, has been a part of human experience throughout time. The yearning for completion that drove that ancient poet to please his beloved drives us to improve our lawns or our aluminum siding, she says. "Sad as it seems, human beings have always been unhappy with who they are. Even the most comely of us feel like eternally ugly ducklings who yearn to be transformed into swans. . . . Regardless of talent, looks, or good fortune, we feel ourselves to be inadequate and in need of some extra genius or flair or energy or serenity" (A *Natural History of Love*, 11–12).

Our possession of brains that can imagine a state of perfection we cannot achieve is, Ackerman concludes, one of the bad jokes of human nature.

Is this persistent longing just a cruel trick, or might there be more to it than that? French physicist and philosopher Blaise Pascal suggested, "There is a God-shaped vacuum in the heart of every person which cannot be satisfied by any created thing, but only by God, the Creator." If the hole that remains, that neediness we still feel no matter how we try to rid ourselves of it, is truly God-shaped, then no wonder the other things we stuff into it fail to satisfy. In fact, we can consider ourselves fortunate that the soul-hunger persists.

M. Scott Peck applies this perspective to an analysis of alcoholism. Some people have a particularly strong hunger for God, he proposes. Feeling on a regular basis an intensity of need that others don't typically experience, they are seekers. When they find alcohol before they find God, they may get stuck for a time. Nonetheless, Peck insists, if they turn from drinking and return to their true pursuit, such seekers are often able to make the deepest connection once they find Deity.

From this vantage point, our usual goals can lose their appeal, not as evils in and of themselves, but as short-circuiters of a greater good. We see our more superficial appetites for what they are: hijackers threatening to take hostage our deepest desire. C. S. Lewis expressed it well: "Our desires [are] not too strong, but too weak. We are half-hearted creatures, fooling about with drink and sex and ambition when infinite joy is offered us, like an ignorant child who wants to go on making mud pies in a slum because he cannot imagine what is meant by the offer of a holiday at the sea. We are far too easily pleased" (*Weight of Glory*, 3–4).

From this perspective, we are willing to undergo deprivation because it deepens our desires. We are willing to live with the longings and yearnings that result when we forgo immediate gratification, not because we are masochistic but because we know this approach will result in an even deeper satisfaction in the long run.

Our everyday cravings are unrelenting precisely because they are fueled by a deeper source. Like waves they break continually along the shore of our consciousness because our hunger is not only for food, our thirst not only for beverage. Gratification can remove our lacking and longing only temporarily. Inevitably the tide recedes and the "cravings of the soul" return. Human limitations snap back into place, and our sense of "not enough" returns. The recurring nature of this struggle can be a source of frustration or motivation. If we are wise, this lacking becomes an impetus for our spiritual seeking. Instead of settling for pain-killers or distractions that temporarily pacify our discomfort, our spirit prods us to keep returning to God in search of the balm that can fill the hole in our soul.

Next time you experience a craving that seems to originate from a need for something simple or superficial, don't immediately flip on the car radio or run to the refrigerator for a snack. Instead, see if you can trace the bubbles back below the surface and down to a deeper source. Next time you feel a sense of discomfort that seems difficult to address or even define, consider the possibility that these are the pangs of soul hunger. Don't pacify them or distract yourself. Instead, tolerate that state of emptiness and even allow your hunger to deepen, so that when you turn to God it will be with open arms and an open heart.

15 Heeding the Voice of Conscience

The voice of conscience is so delicate that it is easy to stifle it; but it is also so clear that it is impossible to mistake it.
—Madame de Stael

"I feel upset when tabloid TV shows run that clip of Tom Cruise and Nicole Kidman making love nude in front of a mirror in the . . . movie *Eyes Wide Shut*. Scenes like that usually don't bother me. Why does this one?" This question was posed to celebrity columnist Walter Scott by a reader in the 13 June 1999 issue of *Parade* magazine (p. 2). Scott gave a well-reasoned answer: We know most actors fake the love scenes; perhaps because these two are married, the scene seems "too real" to us. I think it is unfortunate, however, that apparently neither Scott nor the reader considered the possibility that such discomfort might be the soul's way of warning us that spiritual degradation is occurring. We cannot willingly witness the sacred being treated cheaply without undergoing adverse effects. Whenever we take a step deeper into degeneracy, our sensitivity is deadened a bit, and that leaves us feeling uncomfortable. It leaves us feeling somehow bereft, distinctly less than we were before.

Shortly after leaving home to study at Cambridge, John Wesley, the young student who would later found the Methodist church, wrote a letter home asking his mother how he could best judge which pastimes were acceptable and which "temptations" he should resist. Rather than a list of "do's" and "don'ts," his mother pointed him back to the guidance that could come from his own responses to the various activities he was exploring:

> *Would you judge the lawfulness of pleasure, take this rule:*
> *Whatever weakens your reason,*
> *Whatever increases the authority of your body over your mind,*
> *Whatever impairs the tenderness of your conscience,*

Whatever takes away your relish for things spiritual,
Whatever obscures your sense of God,
That is sin to you, no matter how innocent it may seem in itself.
(Harmer, A War We Must Win, 136)

If desensitization is as widespread and devastating a problem as it seems, then we need to make a high priority of observing the subtle, internal effects of our choices so that we can catch it early in the process and reverse its effects. Fortunately, quiet responses within us do provide clues when we are beginning to become desensitized. An inner soul voice may instill a feeling of discomfort, underscore quiet words of warning from a loved one, or provide a sense of alarm when we are reminded of our former personal standards of decency and can see how they are beginning to slacken. If we hope to retain our capacity to enjoy life to the fullest, we must heed these warning signs and do an "about face" rather than ignore them and continue along the deadening path.

Often, spiritual impressions feel good. When they do, we can respond by going further in the direction that feels right, responding to that quiet but compelling inner voice that tells us we're on the right track. However, the withdrawal of positive feelings, the subtle fading of our sensitivity, can also be a form of guidance. We can be inspired in this way to know when we're starting down the wrong track. Heeding this sort of "negative guidance" can be more of a challenge.

Doug Wright, the host of a local radio station's Friday afternoon *Movie Show*, was discussing the week's new films with three other critics. As they reviewed the first one, he made a confession I've never heard from a movie critic: He had not watched the entire movie. He was offended by the content, to the extent that he stood up and walked out.

"I didn't like what the movie was doing to me," he admitted, "inducing sexual feelings for a girl who was young enough she could have been my daughter. I decided that I didn't want to subject myself to that experience; I didn't want those images staying with me afterward. So I made the decision to leave."

Driving down the freeway listening to my car radio, I cheered and pumped my fist in the air when I heard him describe that act of courage. The next caller expressed what I was feeling, and thanked him for being frank about his response to the film. "I must be out of touch," the caller then said, "because I'm offended by quite a few of the movies reviewers just rave about." Doug Wright suggested that critics see so many movies that perhaps their responsiveness does get blunted. Material that the occasional moviegoer finds stimulating enough might be intolerably routine to the average critic. By the same token, content a critic finds stimulating may overwhelm more sensitive viewers.

One of the *Movie Show* critics who had given the movie a high rating then spoke up. "I liked the movie because it made me feel *something*. That's the criteria by which I judge a movie—does it make me emote." After learning what I have relayed about desensitization, I must admit that comments like that send a chill down my spine. Has this person no idea of what he might be doing to the machinery he depends on for his enjoyment? Although this reviewer may be "in touch" with popular culture, he may be losing touch with his inner soul voice. On the other hand, the caller who felt "out of touch" may be more in touch than he realizes.

Perhaps by now most people have heard about the Leopard Green Frog's fatal flaw: If you place him in a pan of cool water on a stove, and then gradually turn up the heat, the critter will never recognize that the water is getting dangerously hot and will remain in the pan to die. This illustration is often used as a metaphor for desensitization. Once we have submerged below the surface of moral degeneracy and are sinking to its depths, we may no longer have the sense to stop ourselves, so dulled will our conscience have become. We must learn a lesson from the frog and "leap from the pan" at the earliest sign of deadening patterns.

Another, less often recognized lesson from the frog illustration can also be taken. The frog's fatal flaw is actually its very adaptive capacity to adjust to its surroundings. The frog is cold-blooded; its body temperature increases or decreases as the temperature of its environment changes. Similarly, as humans our spiritual and moral "temperature" will often adjust to the level of our environment unless we maintain effective barriers. We cannot willingly submerge ourselves in environments characterized by vulgarity, cynicism, and disregard for the sanctity of life without endangering our own sensitivity. Our attempts to live a higher life will fail if we become complacent and consider ourselves immune to the power of the degrading influences that surround us.

Comfort can be very deceptive. I read not long ago about Hie Kerdchoochuay, a snake charmer in Bangkok who had helped capture a python that had made its way into a neighbor's home. He successfully nabbed the snake, put it into a sack, and was carrying it home when he was stopped by some curious villagers who asked to see the animal. Once he had removed it from the bag, the snake wrapped itself around his neck. Hie screamed for help as the reptile slowly cut off his ability to breathe, but it was too late. Once it had its hold, the python continued to tighten its grip, and soon Hie fell unconscious to the ground. By the time the snake could be unwrapped from his neck, Hie was dead.

As I work with people who have lost their sensitivity to the point that they can no longer enjoy regular life, over and over again they tell me that they never intended to pursue their particular addiction nearly as far as they actually have. Initially they simply wanted to explore, but over time they got comfortable with the activity, and before they knew it, a habit had taken hold. Desensitization, like the deadly python, does not release its prey easily once it has a firm grasp.

Tragically, too often we ignore the initial indications that degrading forces are making their way into our lives. At first, it takes effort to banish the early warning signs from our consciousness. But not for long. Tragically, once ignored, these signs fade more rapidly until, before long, we can no longer discern their message. Then, having ignored the first signs of filth, eventually we can be swamped with it, having taken on so much that our craft is no longer buoyant, the environment within it no longer any safer than the environment without.

Pay attention to the subtle emotional responses you have to the activities you pursue, the shows you watch, and the music you listen to in the coming weeks and months. Ask yourself: What effect are these activities and this material having on me? Does my spirit remain as sensitive as it has been in the past? Judge any activity, even seemingly innocent ones, by asking yourself the questions John Wesley's mother suggested to him: Does this increase the authority of my body over my mind? Does this impair the tenderness of my conscience? Does this take away my relish for things spiritual? Does this obscure my sense of God?

16 Protecting Enjoyment's Machinery

Your body is precious. It is your vehicle for awakening.
Treat it with care.
    —Buddha

One of my clients described during a group therapy session a "wonderful" evening he had had at home with his family. "I rode the exercise bike as my wife and I talked, and then afterwards she rode it and we talked some more." Then he laughed and said, "That sounds so simple, but it really was nice." This kind of joy caught my friend by surprise because just a few months earlier he would never have dreamed that such an uneventful evening could have been enjoyable at all. He had been desensitized to the point where very little but the most intense sexual fantasy and behavior brought him much pleasure. However, once he extracted himself from the intensity trap and began standing up to desire, he was gradually able to recover his sensitivity and thus his ability to enjoy more fully the simple things in life.

This man was reaping the rewards of the suffering he had been tolerating for months. He had survived the dry time, the "disappointment or anticlimax" C. S. Lewis says occurs on the threshold of every worthwhile human endeavor. "It occurs when the boy who has been enchanted in the nursery by Stories from the Odyssey buckles down to really learning Greek. It occurs when lovers have got married and begin the real task of learning to live together. In every department of life it marks the transition from dreaming aspiration to laborious doing" (*Screwtape Letters*, 13). My client had settled into laborious doing and had come to accept more of the drab, real parts of life that his addiction was originally designed to avoid. He had put up with withdrawal symptoms in hopes that his life would be rich and full if he patiently tolerated that seemingly bland existence and worked to restore his sensitivity. Now he was discovering that his capacity to appreciate life was rising to new levels.

"At this point, you need to beware," I warned my client. "In this heightened state of sensitivity, a return to your addiction can be more pleasurable than ever."

He thought about that for a moment. "Right," he responded, "but then my sense of appreciation would be trashed again almost immediately. I'm going to safeguard it more closely than that."

When we truly cherish pleasure, we will not squander it in ways that decrease its future likelihood. Instead, as my friend did, we will protect enjoyment's machinery like sentinels would an important gateway, always remaining vigilant to desensitization and its ability to rob us of our capacity for pleasure. Given the importance of this skill, I think it will be helpful to consider a few examples of how we can stay on guard.

Shortly after my seven-year-old son, Ryan, had returned home from school one afternoon, he came to me for a second opinion. He was holding the family mascot, a guinea pig originally named Snowball but now affectionately known simply as Ginny. "His squeak is different," Ryan reported, obviously concerned.

I listened closely. Sure enough, Ginny was squeaking. But then, he always squeaked when Ryan held him. And I couldn't tell a difference between the squeak the little creature was emitting then and his usual squeak.

"It's been cold. And Zachary and Mom have been sick. Maybe Ginny is sick too," Ryan concluded.

"Maybe he'll feel better if you snuggle him for a while," I suggested.

Half an hour later, Ryan called from his bedroom, "Dad, will you please bring Ginny some lettuce?" I peered over the edge of Ryan's top bunk to see him cuddling the little brown and white creature as I handed him the green leaf. When I was summoned for a second helping a few minutes later, Ryan was smiling. "His squeak is back to normal!"

As I listened again, I could detect that a slight rasp was now gone from his squeak. Ryan was right. "What was different about his squeak before?" I asked Ryan, curious now about what his attentive ears had picked up.

"His throat was clogged up or something," Ryan said. "His voice was different." And then he smiled, "But there's nothing to worry about now!"

We had originally purchased Ginny for a very specific reason. We had received a Nintendo game as a hand-me-down from one of Ryan's uncles when he got a newer version. We had purchased Ryan a game he was excited about, and that was the only game cartridge we had. "Mega-Man X" was a little boy in a bright blue outfit who ran around making his way over obstacles and fighting various opponents. The game seemed harmless enough to us when we purchased it, and Ryan surely enjoyed playing. But one day as I was watching Ryan play, I heard him repeating the words, "I killed him . . . I killed him . . . I killed him" as he summarily dispensed of some minor opponents that stood in his pathway.

That incident disturbed me, and the words Ryan repeated as he played reverberated in my mind. Jenny and I had talked about buying a pet for the kids to take care of, but it had seemed like such a hassle: the smell, the mess, the cost of food, the cleaning of the cage. But at that moment I decided that I would much rather deal with these hassles and have Ryan playing with something real, saying to himself as he fed and took care of a creature, "I kept it alive . . . I kept it alive . . . I kept it alive." We put the Nintendo away that day and took a trip to the pet store that weekend.

As I walked out of Ryan's room after the "squeaking incident," I was so glad we had gotten the guinea pig. Ryan was becoming more sensitive, able to detect a minute difference that signaled changes in the welfare of his little friend. My heart was warm with the assurance that we had done something to stem the tide of desensitization in our home.

Some time ago I heard the story of a young couple who took similar steps to restore their sensitivity once it had been compromised. They took a break from their college studies to take in a movie one Friday night.

Perhaps they chose the wrong film, they decided as they discussed afterward what they had just seen; the portrayal of sexuality and violence had been graphic. In the coming days, they both discovered that images from the movie kept invading their consciousness. The images were compelling, but they left the young woman, in particular, feeling uneasy and troubled.

Most of us have had this experience. What is our typical response to it? Most of the time we simply go on with our lives. We may mentally or verbally acknowledge our mistake, but rarely do we do anything about it. In fact, we may make similar mistakes again and again, chalking them up to "how bad movies have become these days" or the inadequacies of the motion picture industry's rating system. Each time we do so, we submit ourselves to an additional turn in the intensity trap. Thereafter, graphic scenes are a little less disturbing to our dulled sensibilities, even if they are no less memorable and influential.

However, instead of just dismissing the effect that this movie had had on them, brushing it off as something that was now over and done with, this couple took action to stem the tide of desensitization in their lives. They sought out Steve McGary, a professor at their college who shared their religious faith and whose judgment and spiritual sensitivity they trusted, and asked him for a spiritual blessing. He blessed the young woman that the Spirit would be with her, that as she remained faithful to what she knew she should do, her mind would be cleansed of the filth it had been exposed to. He pleaded with God to banish the images from her mind, to protect her from the evil that sought her destruction. The promises of that blessing were realized, and the peace this young woman longed for returned once again to her heart.

A final example is that of John Harmer, an attorney with a distinguished career as a public servant. He was lieutenant governor of California under Ronald Reagan and a California state senator. In his book *A War We Must Win*, Harmer describes the role he has played in the crusade against pornography, a personal effort that has spanned more than three decades. He tells how, in the midst of this effort, he realized at one point that his own spiritual sensitivity was fading, having been deadened by the content of the explicit material he was constantly exposed to in his political work.

> *During one of the series of court battles . . . there came a time when I was feeling alienated from that which was clean and wholesome. I found myself critical of my loved ones and judgmental of other members of [my community and church]. I was negative in my heart toward much and to that which I knew was in harmony with the will of God. I experienced a sense of bitterness toward heaven and life, and an inner arrogance that began to manifest itself by contemptible thoughts about others. Prayer was not the meaningful moment of peaceful communion that it had been. The solace and the comfort that had accompanied my religious observances in the past were no longer being received.*
>
> *I had never become involved in any of the deviant sexual conduct that pervades pornography. I had never compromised my covenants or violated the commandments about chastity. Yet a darkness had come into my mental and spiritual being. One day a comment from my wife made me stop and look more closely into my spiritual mirror. When I did so with an open mind and a sincere prayer to "see things as they really are," . . . I became painfully aware of the "thick darkness" that had gathered around me. (Harmer, A War We Must Win, 143)*

Once he acknowledged his predicament, made an accurate appraisal of the state of his spiritual health, and recognized what was at risk, Harmer sought help and advice. A trusted friend advised him to continue to battle pornography while returning often and for extended periods to a sanctuary where he had previously found peace and comfort. After weeks of quiet worship, fasting, prayer, scripture study, and "laboring in the

Spirit," Harmer fondly recalls the day he finally felt cleansed. He would continue his antipornography work for years without ever again descending into the spiritual darkness that had held him for a time.

A common thread that runs through each of the examples we have considered is worthy of repeated emphasis. Recognizing the dimming of an internal emotional and spiritual light is only part of the solution. Once recognized, the growing darkness cannot be dismissed or tolerated. We must instead immediately chase it from our lives.

In each case we've explored, the identification of the problem—the recognition that desensitization had begun—was only the first step toward resolution and healing. Initially there was concern over a child's response to a violent video game. There was the dysphoria that followed in the wake of an offensive movie. There was the comment of a loving spouse. But these kinds of events alone do not guarantee the outcome of the process. That can be determined only by our own response to these spiritual flares. Every warning like this that we receive in our lives is essentially a call to repentance, as backward and dogmatic as that term may sound given our current culture of openness and tolerance. I think the word fits because, as Ezekiel described it, repentance is but a turning from spiritual death to life (see Ezekiel 18:32).

If we wish to stem the tide of desensitization, we must never allow ourselves to get comfortable in its early, seemingly mild and innocent stages. Instead, we must heed every red flag as a call to "turn ourselves, and live." It is our heeding and responding, and not the signal itself, that can once again restore our peace and return us to safety. The quiet voice of our conscience and the wisdom of those we trust will help us chart out our course back to higher ground. We may be led to study holy scripture or other spiritual writings, engage in religious rituals of meditation and purification, simply walk out of a movie, or perhaps even get a pet.

Become more aggressive in guarding your capacity to enjoy life. As you do so, you will likely have to look for alternative forms of entertainment and leisure for you and your family. Spend time reading, watching, and retelling uplifting stories. If you have been desensitized, tolerate the "dry times" associated with withdrawal from intense stimulation as the price you are paying to recover your ability to take pleasure in the richness in life. Seek out spiritual leaders for help in the process and spend time studying and pondering God's word. If you then appreciate your newfound sensitivity as it expands, you will be even more vigilant to safeguard and protect it.

17

Waking Up to the Abundance Right before Us

If there is a sin against life, it consists perhaps not so much in despairing of life as in hoping for another life and in eluding the implacable grandeur of this life.
—Albert Camus

Are you wealthy? I'm not asking whether you *feel* wealthy, but whether you *are* wealthy compared to the rest of the people in the world. In addition to walking, do you have another mode of transportation available to you? Do you own more than one pair of shoes? Do you have variety in your diet—two or more food items available for each meal? Do you have more than one set of underwear? If you answered yes to three or more of those questions, you are better off than 90 percent of all people who have ever lived (Glenn and Nelsen, *Raising Self-Reliant Children,* 44–45).

David Myers tells a story about his friend Ruth, who once worked in a Nigerian village. She recalls watching "a group of five- to seven-year-old boys wearing rags for clothes and racing along our compound's driveway with a toy truck made of tin cans from my trash. They had spent the greater part of a morning engineering the toy—and were squealing with delight as they pushed it with a stick. My sons, with Tonka trucks parked under their beds, looked on with envy" (*Pursuit of Happiness,* 39). These Nigerian children were fully immersed in the enjoyment of what little they had. It amazes me how this kind of immersion can displace all longing and leave no room for self-pity.

Earlier we explored the fact that enjoyment does not come from the raw material of our lives. Now we will look more closely at where it does come from: our outlook regarding what we do have.

On an occasional Sunday afternoon when we were in high school, I would go with my buddies Darin and Dave to a nursing home that was a short drive from our neighborhood. It was known as "the convalescent center" at the time, which struck us as ironic because most of the residents there were not very responsive and seemed to be on their way toward death rather than recovery. Because the overall environment of the center seemed depressing to us, I'll never forget the talks we had with Marvus, a long-time resident who was unable to take care of most of her own basic needs due to the crippling effects of the polio she had suffered as a child.

From the first day we walked into her room, it was obvious to us that Marvus was special. She flashed a bright smile, called out a cheery "hello," and invited us in to chat. My friends and I had come to help lift the spirits of those we visited, but we quickly learned that we were the ones who left the center uplifted by Marvus's enthusiasm and vivaciousness.

One day when we arrived to see her, we could tell by her fallen countenance that Marvus wasn't her usual lively self. She admitted to us that she had been feeling troubled throughout the day. "I've just been thinking," she said, "of all the unfortunate people who don't believe in God, who don't know in their hearts that he loves them. He cherishes them, but they don't know it, and I feel so sorry for them."

I will never forget sitting beside Marvus, her scrawny and virtually useless body propped into a sitting position on her bed, as she described her sympathy for people who didn't share what she held most dear: her optimistic outlook and spiritual foundation. No wonder Marvus was so happy, I thought. If I were in her state, I might be resenting my own plight, but instead she focused on what she had and saved her sorrow for others she felt were in a worse state. As I look back now, I realize that her perspective was in fact quite accurate: Most of us probably are more to be pitied than Marvus.

I am convinced that it's not difficult to appreciate what we have, to wake up to the abundance that is right before us. However, this outlook typically will not sprout on its own. We must cultivate it. Instead of ruminating about what we don't have, we must immerse ourselves, as Marvus did, in the enjoyment of what is available to us. Keeping this perspective may require even more effort for those of us who are relatively healthy and prosperous because our minds so naturally adapt to the status quo. We must keep reminding ourselves that our sense of "not enough" is an illusion.

When I want to change lanes in traffic, I check my rearview mirror to see if it's safe. I won't merge if I see a car—even if it seems to be several car-lengths behind me. I have read the warning "OBJECTS IN MIRROR ARE CLOSER THAN THEY APPEAR" often enough to have trained myself to figure this distortion into my calculations and decision making. Things are not always as they appear, but such distortions in our perception can have no power over us if we remain alert to their operation.

We would do well to carry a similar warning around with us in our heads, keeping it superimposed on our view of the raw material of our lives: "OBJECTS IN VIEW ARE MUCH BETTER THAN THEY APPEAR."

I have heard pilots say that the optical illusions they sometimes experience are so powerful that they must play tricks on themselves in order to "correct" their vision. They have to resist the tendency to respond as it appears they should and make themselves respond as their instruments direct. Since we know that our highly adaptable minds are playing tricks on us, blinding us to the abundance right before us, perhaps we should also play tricks on ourselves to reverse such distortions and restore a more realistic outlook. I love the restorative, attitude-correcting tricks suggested by author Timothy Miller:

> *When you wash the dog, try pretending it is the only surviving member of an otherwise extinct species. When you urinate, pretend you are a urologist, knowledgeable and curious about every urinary tract sensation and structure. When you watch TV, pretend you have recently arrived from another planet where nothing like TV exists. When you eat cornflakes, imagine that you have just emerged from a dungeon where you*

spent twenty years with nothing to eat but maggoty gruel and muddy water. (How to Want What You Have, 150)

The abundance is right there before us. We may be blind to it now, but the fact that it has disappeared from our view does not mean that it has departed. We can correct our vision if we work at it, and ultimately we can restore our view.

Begin right away to more fully appreciate what you have. As a starting point, you may use the little vision-correcting mind games Timothy Miller suggests (above). Discipline yourself to think more about what you already have instead of what you want. Recall the times when you wished for what you now have: your car, your home, those shoes, that new set of tools. Counting your blessings in a gratitude journal can be another powerful means of keeping the abundance that is right before you in full view and in sharp focus. Giving away some of your abundance to others who have less—and then watching how much they appreciate it—can also have a powerful restorative effect on your outlook.

18

Enjoyment's Paradoxical Pace

Happiness is the harvest of a quiet eye.
—Austin O'Malley

Ours is a culture of instant gratification. We can order almost any product and get it within days or even by overnight mail. We respond with a sense of entitlement to a pharmaceutical company's complaint that the ten minutes their competitor's popular pain reliever takes to start working is too long. Take a moment to assess your own tolerance for inconvenience. Admit honestly: Have you ever been irritated when . . .

- your e-mail or internet connection takes a few extra seconds to boot up?
- road construction requires that you take a three-minute detour?
- you misdial the last digit of a phone number and have to redial the entire number again?
- you have to wait in line for ten minutes to get your fast food from a drive-through window?
- you can't find the TV remote control and have to get up from the couch to change the channel?
- as you enter a building, you are one step too slow and have to wait for the next section of a revolving door?
- the airplane you are on, which will get you to your destination in one-tenth of the time it would take to drive, must taxi for ten minutes before taking off?

Let's take a few minutes to consider this strange state of affairs and how we arrived at this point. Our pace is increasing all the time, and yet we are less satisfied than ever with what we are able to get done in an hour, in an afternoon, in a day.

How could this be? The key is in understanding that hurrying can act as bait that leads us into the intensity trap. The immediate and long-term effects of hurrying are contradictory, just as the immediate and long-term effects of accruing or obtaining can be. In an immediate sense, the experience seems to go like this: Some process is boring or onerous, so we try to get it over with more quickly. When we improve our efficiency in some way, thereby cutting some of the time required for performing the task, we experience a sense of relief. Therefore, we assume that continuing to shave time by using a new technology or more efficient method will bring even greater contentment. However, that is not the way it works in the long run.

On a typical afternoon a century ago, our great-grandparents likely picked vegetables from their gardens, brought them into the kitchen, chopped them, and put them with some meat stock into a pot of water. To get the stewing process started, they placed the pot on top of a stove they had stoked with coals and lit earlier in the afternoon. Within a couple of hours the family would be sitting down to eat.

Since that time we've seen improvements in the efficiency of the processes we use to grow, prepare, and cook our food. Let's imagine that our ancestors may have experienced something between slight irritation and extreme aggravation as they prepared dinner. Well, with the help of grocery stores, food processors, and gas or electric heat sources we have so reduced the hassle, time, and effort we put into fixing a meal that today we should be in a state close to Nirvana by the time we eat. Instead, our impatience has grown in tandem with our efficiency. We can hardly stand to make things from scratch now, and we even tap our feet impatiently as we wait for the beep of the microwave to signal that our instant meal is ready.

In contrast with the immediate effect of small increases in our speed and efficiency, the cumulative influence of many such changes seems to have been to undermine our peace of mind instead of fostering it.

Gandhi taught simply, "There is more to life than turning up the speed." It seems that we have forgotten this simple truth in our modern lives. I've heard it said that in an earlier generation, when people missed a stagecoach, they didn't get too upset—after all, another one would be by in a few days! Now we lose our temper if the driver in front of us slows down and makes us miss a green traffic light.

Will Durant said, "No man who is in a hurry is quite civilized." Interestingly enough, the most civilized part of the brain does tend to shut down when we arouse ourselves in an effort to get more done in less time. In times of stress, the cortex—the outer shell of the brain responsible for rationality and self-control—can be overridden more easily by impulses from the brain core that are aggressive, sexual, and otherwise self-destructive. Drivers who commit acts of "road rage" often turn out to be people who are quite civil by reputation. It is not unusual to hear them report after such incidents that they have been under a lot of pressure lately. Similarly, every now and then a case hits the news of a respected member of the community propositioning a prostitute. As I have worked with people who are trying to overcome addictions to substances, sexual behavior, food, and the accrual of possessions through spending or shoplifting, my clients and I have discovered that relapses to their self-destructive behavior almost always occur during times of stress.

Although we may think that we are increasing our productivity when we are always pushing ourselves to get more done, we enjoy life more and are actually more productive when we allow ourselves to cycle between times of exertion and output on the one hand and times of quiet relaxation and restoration on the other (Rossi, *Twenty-Minute Break*). I realize that this kind of advice may seem counterproductive, so steeped are we in a cultural climate that promises the most for those who do the most. In truth, we are invigorated and even better prepared to work after we have taken a break to fly a kite or simply to relax and enjoy the scenery from our window for a few moments.

All it takes is a few moments of relaxation to slow our brainwaves from the fast-paced beta waves to the rejuvenating alpha waves. Our consumption of oxygen decreases, and our bodies are better able to metabolize stress hormones like cortisol and adrenaline. In fact, our autonomic nervous systems even shift from the "fight or flight" mode into the slower-paced "feed or breed" mode. No wonder our enjoyment is so dependent on our pace. Whenever I work with couples who have lost their sexual desire, I teach them about the effect of stress on the body's autonomic nervous system. Sometimes their enjoyment of sexual intimacy is restored by their simply making fewer demands on themselves, reducing the stress in their lives.

I once heard Dr. Bernie Siegel tell a story about the surprising payoff that giving up our frenetic pace can bring. One day he received the news that his father was dying. "It's time to come see Dad," he was told. "It looks like this may be our last visit with him."

"Before learning the value of quiet pondering, I would have hurriedly packed my bags and rushed to the airport," Segal recalled. "Instead, the first thing I did was sit down and meditate, just contemplating Dad and the good life he had lived. Taking that time put me in a completely different frame of mind. When I arrived at his bedside the next day, instead of 'How are you feeling?' I asked, 'Dad, how did you and Mom meet?' We had a wonderful conversation, and my dad died with a smile on his face, all because I had taken the time to tune in to what really mattered."

My mother-in-law, Sandra Brown, has described how she learned the importance of slowing down to appreciate life as a young adolescent at girl's camp. She was in a group of girls returning from a hike in the majestic Teton mountains. Their guide for the day had been Fred Miller, a mountaineer and master teacher who had spent countless hours in those mountains helping fellow campers, reciting poetry and singing with them, tutoring them, and simply enjoying their company. Miller was especially fond of young hikers who were new to the mountains. Most of the girls hurried to the end of the trail, but a few—my mother-in-law among them—hung back to enjoy Fred Miller's company. He encouraged them to pause and then asked them to close their eyes and listen to the sunset.

"I wasn't sure what he meant, but I closed my eyes as he began to point out all the sounds, smells, and sensations in the forest at dusk. He began to teach us what it meant to enjoy the mountains, not just get to the end. I knew that day that I had met someone who was going to have a profound effect on my life," she recalled at his funeral. "In fact, he couldn't get rid of us from that day on."

Next time you feel like you just don't have enough, and are tempted to go about busily seeking more and more of those things you think will lead to fulfillment, pause and consider your ways. You may truly have no need for any more stimulation than you already have. For it is against a daily backdrop of muted color and subdued detail that periodic gems of experience stand out in most bold relief.

When we willingly go into a quiet life, we will discover that below the din of typical life there is a magnificence to some of our more sublime experiences that cannot be rivaled by the flash of fireworks or the blare of rock concerts. Often, we can increase our chances of participating in these kinds of experiences by simply slowing down and tuning in.

19

Cultivating Awareness

As to me, I know of nothing else but miracles.
—Walt Whitman

Carleen comes home from work for lunch. She fixes herself some rice and gravy with a salad on the side and sits down to eat her meal. She thinks, *It's so nice to relax. Let's see what's on TV.* She picks up the remote control and switches on the set. She watches the local noon news program as she eats, enjoying the distraction from her day at work. Finishing her meal, she leaves the house to return to work. *It was good to get away for lunch,* she thinks as she drives toward her office, and she begins mentally sorting through the tasks she must complete that afternoon. As she arrives back at the office, she makes a quick stop at the rest room, rushing back to her desk just in time to resume her workday.

Sound like a typical lunch hour? Nothing unusual, you say? But think about it for a moment. Perhaps there has been no other time in history when people have taken food—and the privilege of having enough to eat—so for granted that they considered time spent eating to be "dead time." It is sad that we have become so accustomed to having enough to eat that we no longer consider a full plate deserving of our full attention! Isn't there enough going on with our own bodies to keep us busy as we eat? The taste of the chicken gravy, the texture of the rice and chunks of chicken meat in her mouth. The snap of celery, the tangy vinaigrette dressing with spicy bursts of flavor from the ground pepper. The satisfaction of a filling stomach. The truth is, there is enough to keep us occupied during a typical meal. Unfortunately, we have worked ourselves into such a frenzy, tried to pack our lives so full of stimulation, that when we slow down to eat, it seems as though just eating is not enough, that we need to be doing more.

The typical person, the great Leonardo da Vinci observed, "looks without seeing, listens without hearing, touches without feeling, eats without tasting, moves without physical awareness, inhales without awareness of odor or fragrance, and talks without thinking." If da Vinci's lament was an accurate characterization of the way people in his time lived, it is even more true today.

Instead of being aware, too often we go through the motions of our lives in a trance. Once we have learned and then practiced the steps for completing a given task, the habit system in our brains can carry out that task without the participation of our conscious attention. Our ability to complete many activities in this autopilot mode is a tremendously efficient skill; unfortunately, many of us are living like zombies, with the autopilot almost constantly in the driver's seat.

How much do we miss simply because we are not aware of it? "If we had keen vision and feeling for all ordinary human life," wrote nineteenth-century author Mary Ann Evans under the pen name George Eliot, "it would be like hearing the grass grow and the squirrel's heart beat, and we should die of the roar which lies on the other side of silence. As it is, the quickest of us walks about well wadded with stupidity" (Breathnach, *Simple Abundance*, April 22).

A Zen master was once approached by a curious outsider and asked how he and his followers managed to live in such peace and contentment. "What is your secret?" the man inquired.

The Zen master answered simply, "We sit . . . we eat . . . we walk."

"But that cannot be," the man objected, "for I also sit, I eat, and I walk. And yet my life is not satisfying."

"But when we sit," the master responded, "we are aware that we are sitting. When we eat, we are aware that we are eating. When we walk, we are aware that we are walking."

This is a possibility we don't usually consider: that we may not need to do any more than we are doing, but rather should simply attend in a more disciplined way to the input we already take in through our senses.

Initially dabbling in photography as a hobby, through practice and study my brother, Darrel, has developed considerable skill and has produced some beautiful work. When I asked him whether he has developed more visual sensitivity with practice, he told me, "I can now tell in the morning what kind of sunset we might see that evening." When I asked how this capacity evolved, he described days upon days of sitting and observing, watching the changes in light and color that occur second by second, minute by minute, hour by hour. As we talked, I was amazed at all the subtle cues he had learned to interpret. "Now I can see the elements that create a rainbow coming together before the colors appear," he said. "At times I have had just enough time to pull over if I'm driving and get out my camera to capture it on film."

Some massage therapists are given a penny and a phone book as a part of their training. Initially they place the penny underneath a few dozen pages. They then run their hands and fingers across the top page to practice finding the small, almost imperceptible lump made by the penny. Once they become familiar with that sensation, they move the penny several dozen more pages deeper. Their practice continues and their sensitivity increases. Very quickly they are able to sense with their fingers subtle surface irregularities that the rest of us could not, irregularities they themselves could not have detected just a short time before. This sensitivity allows them to better diagnose as they provide treatment, finding and easing the "knots" in the muscles of their clients.

It is fitting that we refer to massage therapy and photography as disciplines, for that is exactly what is required to increase one's skill in either—discipline. It is as true of skilled car mechanics and radiologists as it is of photographers and massage therapists: They can see and feel and hear things the rest of us miss because they have invested time and effort in their respective disciplines. Any improvement in our ability comes at the price of time, effort, patience, and receptivity.

The power and rewards of disciplining oneself to become more aware

were demonstrated in a profound way by the late psychiatrist Milton
Erickson. His story is worth telling in some detail.

When he was seventeen years old, Milton was stricken with polio.
Almost immediately, his condition deteriorated to the point that his doctor predicted he would not live through the night. Upon hearing this,
Milton vowed that he would see another sunset. He requested that the
dresser be moved and its mirror be positioned in such a way that he would
have an unobstructed view of the next day's sunset through the west window of the house. He was exhilarated when the sunset finally came, but
then collapsed into a state of unconsciousness.

Instead of dying, however, he regained consciousness three days later
and began the slow and arduous process of recovery. But his body would
never be the same. He lost use of almost all his muscles and was completely dependent on others for his care. His family ran a farm and was
struggling to make ends meet, so there was little time for them to wait on
Milton. Before they would leave to work in the morning, they would
place him in a rocking chair with a hole cut through the seat so that it
acted as a toilet as well. He was tied in the chair so that he wouldn't fall
from it during the day. He would have company again when they returned
for lunch, and then spend the afternoon on his own in that chair again.

Put yourself in Milton's situation. Every one of us can relate to him
in some small way. How do you react when you are forced to wait, with
nothing to do? Think about what it's like to wait for a haircut, for a car
repair, for your appointment at the doctor's office, or for someone you're
running errands with to return to the car. I remember waiting in the car as
a boy while my mom ran errands. I'm not proud to admit that when she
took longer than I expected, I would usually work myself into a mental
frenzy and then whine at her when she got back to the car. I'm even more
embarrassed to admit that I sometimes still react that way when I have to
wait.

Consider how different Milton's response was. He spent countless hours gazing out the window, simply observing, taking the time to see things he had never noticed before. As he attended to the faintest of sights and sounds, his perceptual abilities were sharpened. From the house, Milton would hear the barn door close. He attended to clues indicating the manner in which it had been closed. He would then consider the sound of that person's footsteps from the barn to the door of the house. He considered the way that the door was opened and closed as the person entered the house, and the clues regarding other movements once the person was in the house. In this way, he came to better know his family members' personalities and moods.

Lacking other opportunities, Milton constantly worked to refine his observational powers during his young adulthood and throughout his career as a psychiatrist. Early on, he became a student of his toddler sister as she crawled, stood, and then finally walked, watching her movements and the contracting of her muscles and reliving in his own mind what it felt like to make these simple movements. He passed some of his time reliving his favorite sensory pleasures from earlier years: climbing a tree, swinging from its branches, and feeling the soil against his feet as he walked through a freshly plowed field.

Deprived of the usual physical outlets, Milton's imaginative powers were expanding. One day, no one in his family remembered to move him over to the window before they left for their morning work. As a result, he was left with nothing but a closed door as his view for half the day.

> Milton . . . wanted to look out or go out so badly that he began looking intently at the door and remembering how it used to feel to put pressure from his hands on the arms of the chair and walk to the door and go outside. He did this as precisely as his memory would allow. He recalled each muscular movement that would allow him to rise from the chair and walk. Then he noticed that the rocking chair began to rock ever so slightly. Somehow his paralyzed body was able to make small twitches

and get the chair to rock. Milton was accessing and activating old physiological patterns for movement. It was at this moment that Milton Erickson began to realize that if he was capable of making random twitches that could cause the chair to move, he could learn how to make these twitches deliberate and someday move, if not walk again. (Sylvester, "Milton H. Erickson, M.D.," 284–85)

Although he never did walk, the imagination and keen observational powers that Milton Erickson honed during those endless hours would later enable him to help many people with their emotional and spiritual struggles. His keen perceptiveness gave him an eye for people's strengths perhaps unmatched by any other mental-health practitioner before or since. He enjoyed people immensely, respected them, and saw them as capable of solving their own problems, often with minimal—although strategically precise—help from him.

For instance, Erickson once worked briefly with a wealthy, fifty-two-year-old spinster who lived alone in her big house in Milwaukee and ventured out only to attend church. Her relatives, concerned that she was so withdrawn, worried that she was depressed and might even be suicidal. Her nephew, who was acquainted with Erickson, asked if he might meet the woman during his next visit to Milwaukee and see if he could somehow help her. Erickson visited the woman in her home. He saw that she led a very quiet and isolated life. However, he also recognized two of her strengths:

She expressed a deep sense of commitment to her church community (even though she didn't actively participate in it), and . . . she grew some beautiful African violet plants in the sunroom of our house. . . . Erickson grew curious about how the latter two values might be used to increase the woman's participation in the community.

He got the woman to agree to raise many more African

violets. He then directed her to give one of these plants to indi-viduals or families in her church community each time they expe-rienced an important transitional event such as a birth, death, illness, marriage, and so on. . . . She followed these instructions and became "too busy to be depressed." Furthermore, she became quite active in the community and earned the apprecia-tion and attention of many people. In fact, when she died over 20 years later, she was mourned and lovingly remembered as the "African Violet Queen of Milwaukee." (Gilligan, "If You Really Knew Me," 288–89)

Using his acute sense of awareness, Erickson honed in on this woman's strengths and then leveraged their motivating power. Eventually they blossomed to fill her own life and brighten the lives of many others. For work such as this, years after his death Milton Erickson is now widely recognized as one of this century's most brilliant revolutionaries in the sci-ence of the mind. From seemingly arid soil, he reaped a rich harvest that continues to feed many simply because he was more aware of what the rest of us usually miss.

Look and listen more closely and see if there are not many things to which you have been blind and deaf before. Expand your ability to enjoy the simple and seemingly mundane aspects of life by attending more closely to them. Next time you take out the garbage, walk from the store to your car, or talk with a familiar person, pay attention and become aware of what you may have been taking for granted. Slow down enough to notice previously ignored sensations and input. Approach the most commonplace aspects of your work with an eye for what you might have been missing.

Sensitivity Breeds Delight

Delight is probably the one thing in the world that may honestly be said to be its own reward.
—Walter Kerr

We have explored the way sensitivity grows as we cultivate our awareness. Now we will examine perhaps the sweetest fruit of disciplined attending: the increase it brings in our capacity for enjoyment. Those who develop a heightened sense of awareness are no longer as dependent on their environment for pleasure. For them, thrills can come not only from amusement-park intensity but from the sublime beauty of a tree, a simple melody, or a bird flying overhead.

Neal A. Maxwell has described treasures that lie on the other side of silence, and promises that once we arrive there, "things which we had never supposed come into view. Seeming routine turns out to be resplendent with possibilities. Ordinary people seem quite the opposite. The humdrum of life, when savored, contains symphonic sounds. A circumstance or conversation which looks quite pedestrian nevertheless proves pivotal. But there are no bands playing, no headlines, no footage on the six o'clock news" (*We Will Prove Them Herewith*, 12–13).

Our moments of most sublime enjoyment, those unforgettable epiphanies that we treasure for years, often involve a heightened sensory awareness. Such an awareness expands our appreciation of even the most commonplace aspects of life as we awaken to the grandeur of the world around us. Consider a couple of illustrations, the first retold by author Walter Kerr:

> *I was walking along a narrow street, which was both old and new, with low houses on either side, all white and tucked away in courtyards or little gardens, with wooden fences, painted . . . pale yellow, was it pale yellow? I was all alone on the street. I was walking along by the fences and the houses, and it was*

fine, not too hot, with the sun above, high above my head in the blue of the sky. I was walking fast, but where was I going? I don't remember. I was deeply aware of the unique joy of being alive. I'd forgotten everything, all I could think of was those houses, that deep sky and that sun, which seemed to be coming nearer, within my grasp, in a world that was made for me. (Decline of Pleasure, *221*)

In a completely different set of circumstances—ascending the sheer cliff of El Capitan in Yosemite—rock climber Yvon Chouinard experienced a similarly expansive sense of joy over small and ordinary things:

Each individual crystal in the granite stood out in bold relief. The varied shapes of the clouds never ceased to attract our attention. For the first time, we noticed tiny bugs that were all over the walls, so tiny that they were barely noticeable. I stared at one for fifteen minutes, watching him move and admiring his brilliant red color.

How could one ever be bored with so many good things to see and feel! This unity with our joyous surroundings, this ultra-penetrating perception, gave us a feeling that we had not had in years. (Csikszentmihalyi, Flow, *205*)

Considering these descriptions, it is not surprising to learn that Michael Gelb has identified *sensazione*—the continual refinement of sensory awareness—as one of the principles that Leonardo da Vinci cherished as essential to the good life (see *How to Think Like Leonardo da Vinci: Seven Steps to Genius Every Day*). Those whose sensitivity is refined can appreciate the beauty of a simple neighborhood on a sunny day or the individual crystals in a block of granite or even the sight of tiny bugs. They do not require large buffet tables to delight their palates; a simple meal is sufficiently stimulating. Author David Lykken describes a conversation he overheard once while sitting in a restaurant:

There were four men at that table, young enough so that it was easy to picture them at their high school graduations not so many years earlier. They were talking with great animation and real interest about a subject that clearly held for them great fascination. Was it sex, the last Vikings football game, was it politics, religion, or how to catch a walleyed pike? No, they were talking about linoleum. They were in the business, you see, and they knew quite a lot about its fine points, prices, new products, profit margins, and installation problems. My thought at the time was how they would have scoffed, at the actual time of their high school graduations, if anyone had told them that a few years hence they would be enthralled by . . . linoleum! But . . . these young men now were enthralled, fascinated by what they'd learned about the linoleum business and optimistic about its prospects. They were not . . . cut off from the enjoyment of their existence by their need to "struggle for life"—they were enjoying the struggle and they were plainly happy. (Happiness, 67–68)

Only when it is approached as a discipline can something as simple and seemingly humdrum as linoleum ignite this kind of passion. Such pleasure in our work comes at a price. Experts in any arena, from linoleum to archeology, experience periods of struggle when their work no longer gives them a "charge." However, instead of abandoning the quest, they stretch themselves by attacking new problems and working to deepen their knowledge and skills.

The process of disciplined attending can evoke rich rewards from processes that may seem at first glance to be the most commonplace and mundane in all of life. Remember Candace Pert, the brain scientist involved in the pioneering research that discovered opiate ligands, the tiny neuropeptide receptors within the cells of the brain and body that allow us to register enjoyment. One fascinating area of work she describes in her book, *Molecules of Emotion*, has been brain scientists' discovery that pleasure receptors are densely clustered in the Nucleus of Barrington, a group of cells in the back of the brain that receives primary input from the bowel and bladder. Practically speaking, this means that the simple operation of the bodily functions we must perform daily can be an enjoyable experience, if we remain aware of the process. The dense concentration of receptors throughout the rest of the digestive system means that tasting food, swallowing, and digesting are all potentially pleasurable experiences. We all know the feelings of satisfaction that can come from eating a good meal. Koreans have a saying that is translated literally, "My stomach is singing." That's an apt description of the subjective state of enjoyment we can experience when an entire chorus of opiate ligands vibrates in sync, sending waves of mild ecstasy through us.

Helen Keller developed an incredible capacity to enjoy an extremely wide range of sensations at astoundingly subtle levels. Her teacher, Annie Sullivan, did much to help Helen experience the world in the ways she still could. She placed an egg in Helen's hand precisely at the moment it was about to hatch. She taught her language by signing rapidly with her fingers into Helen's hand. In order to receive such communication, Helen had to attend to tactile input in a way that very few are ever required to do. She was left to rely upon the subtlest vibrations against her body, slight variations in the texture and contour of objects, and changes in the temperature, movement, and humidity of the air that surrounded her.

We observe in Helen's life, just as in Milton Erickson's, that although sensitivity is one of the most precious fruits deprivation can bring, it does not spring from deprivation's soil spontaneously but must be cultivated in a disciplined way. Without access to the immense array of visual and auditory input that most of us must sort through, Helen's mind grasped for the slightest clues provided by her senses of smell, touch, and taste. As a result of repeatedly practicing disciplined attending, Helen became more aware of and sensitive to the sensory input she did receive. "With the skin of my face and nose I notice different atmospheric conditions according to the season, even at various hours of the same day and in different regions," she wrote. She contrasted the cold sun of wintertime and the air of mid-summer, which could be heavy and damp or dry and burning. She made a distinction between the "vital and fragrant" rain of spring and the chill and odorless storms of fall and winter ("The World through Three Senses," 223).

To Helen, disciplined attending was a necessity, and her sensitivity often paid off in practical ways. She described having her papers blown from her desk by a breeze from an open window. As she jumped to recapture them, amazingly, she was guided to them "by the direction from which their flutter on the rug reaches me."

Her awareness of and empathy for others also deepened as she developed sensitivity through paying attention: "Footsteps vary tactually according to the age, the sex and the manners of the walker. The child's patter is unlike the tread of a grown person. The springy step youth differs from the sedate walk of the middle-aged and from the gait of the old man whose feet drag along the floor. In persons whom I know well I detect many moods and traits in their walk—energy or laziness, firmness or hesitation, weariness, impatience or distress" ("The World through Three Senses," 223).

Helen's reputation for sensitivity became legendary. It is said that, at a party, a receiving line spontaneously formed of people who wanted to meet the famous woman. Before leaving the party, one of the guests who had already been through got in line to shake hands with her again. Keller, it is said, recognized the hand immediately as belonging to the woman she had met earlier.

Given the central role that awareness plays in the experience of enjoyment, it is not surprising that Helen delighted in so many of her life experiences. As we read her writings, we see that her attention to the minute details of the world around her enabled her to savor the depth and richness of life. "Each day comes to me with both hands full of possibilities," she wrote, "and in its brief course I discern all the verities and realities of my existence, the bliss of growth, the glory of action, the spirit of beauty" (*Light in My Darkness*, 34).

Although it may be helpful for us to make a list of the things we have to be grateful for, and to contemplate that list mentally, Helen's descriptions of the bliss, glory, and beauty of existence strike us more as a lover's embrace than an exercise. It is not surprising to hear her enlist the language of romance to describe her relationship with the world that surrounded her:

> *The seasons always charm me as a succession of surprises.*
> *No matter how attentively I watch for their signs, they are never*
> *the same in odor or temperature. One day when I go out to clip*
> *grass it is frosty, and buds on tree and bush are still small and*
> *hard. A few days later I am at my outdoor work again, and lo,*
> *the maples are in leaf, the evergreens are beginning to put out*
> *soft new tips, the turf palpitates with promises of clover and dan-*
> *delion. Soon the rosebushes and lilac trees are aflutter with fra-*
> *grant little leaves that seem to my fingers cool distillations of dew*
> *and air. ("The World through Three Senses," 225)*

Rather than expecting and therefore experiencing the "same old thing" day after day, Helen was tuned into the real world and sensitive to its endless diversity. Rather than insisting that the world fit into her mold, she was willing to meet it on its terms and rediscover it every day. Yet she delighted not only in the novelty of unfamiliar experiences but in the memories that familiar ones could evoke. "Every time I smell daisies I am a radiantly happy little girl in the dew-drenched fields, walking with my teacher," she wrote. She found that scents invited her back in time: "A whiff from a meadow where hay has been cut transports me back to the big New England barn where my little friends and I used to play in a huge haymow." Similarly, "The days brimful of adventure, work and beauty I spent in California return to me whenever I catch the odor of a pepper tree, a eucalyptus or a citrus grove" ("The World through Three Senses," 227).

Clearly, our prospects are better than we could have imagined. If Helen Keller could enjoy life with only three senses, if linoleum experts can be thrilled by their work, if going to the bathroom is all it takes to activate our body's pleasure response, then delight is infinitely available to us. We too can enjoy everyday events and experiences such as these when we work in a disciplined way to cultivate our sensitivity and awareness.

We can more fully appreciate the simple experiences in life by refusing to ignore them any longer. We can stop gobbling down food on the run. We can stop distracting ourselves with a stack of reading material in the bathroom. We can discipline ourselves to tune back in to all of the little things in life that are so easy to take for granted. We can rediscover our sense of awe and reignite our passion for life by appreciating what is available, allowing it to hold our attention and "charm" us. As we take pleasure in these experiences, we will more fully capture the everyday miracle and wonder of being alive.

Delighting In People

*When you have a taste for exceptional people you always
end up meeting them everywhere.*
—Pierre Mac Orlan

One day as I contemplated the wonder of God's creations, I was struck by this realization: I am always on the lookout for beauty in the natural world around me. I can readily enjoy a beautiful scene or the melody of a songbird. So why is it that when it comes to God's highest creation, other human beings, I so often overlook their beauty or, worse yet, focus on what I perceive to be their faults or weaknesses? Surely God enjoys the beauty of my neighbor more than the curb appeal of my neighborhood. The realization that I could do the same has been a transforming one for me. My enjoyment of life has grown as I have begun to exercise more fully my ability to enjoy other people.

I love J. B. S. Haldane's expression: "The world shall perish not for lack of wonders, but for lack of wonder." Perhaps one of the most important applications of this principle concerns our appreciation of other people. In this regard, a slightly altered version of his statement is equally true: We suffer for lack of wonder, and not a lack of wonderful people.

Fortunately, wonder can be cultivated. Jane Goodall immersed herself in the world of the chimpanzees she lived among and studied. She was fascinated by them and carefully observed and documented their movements, their relationships, and the rules of their culture. Watching film footage of her work, you can see how much she enjoyed herself. If we applied Jane Goodall's curiosity in our interactions with our children, our neighbors, our co-workers, and our spouses, imagine what we might discover about them. Imagine how much more we might enjoy them.

Turning again to the life of Helen Keller, our quintessential specialist in the art of appreciation, we are not surprised to discover that she had a knack for enjoying other people. Her pleasure is quite apparent in the

following interview recorded by Ernest Gruening of the *Boston Herald*.
Helen had just spoken at an international conference for Otologists at
Harvard Medical School. Had she known there was a crowd when she
spoke at the Medical School? Gruening asked her.

*"I should say I did," Miss Keller replied. "I could feel them
and smell them."*

"How did you feel them?"

*"By any number of vibrations through the air, and through
the floor, from the moving of feet or the scraping of chairs and
by the warmth when there are people around."*

"How could you tell by your sense of smell?"

"There was a doctor's odor."

*"Do you mean to say that doctors have a special odor which
you can recognize?"*

*"A very decided odor," Miss Keller said. "It's partly the
smell of ether and partly the smell that lingers from the sick rooms
in which they have been. But I can tell many professions from
their odor."*

"Which ones?" I asked.

*"Doctors, painters, sculptors, masons, carpenters, drug-
gists, and cooks."*

"What does the carpenter smell like, and the druggist?"

*"The carpenter is always accompanied by the odor of wood.
The druggist is saturated with various drugs. There is a painter
who comes here often and I can always tell the minute he comes
anywhere near me."*

*"Could you tell my work in that way?" I asked. "Do you
smell any ink?"*

*"No, a typewriter, I think," Miss Keller answered quickly,
laughing.*

"Could you really tell that?"

Miss Keller's rippling laugh continued. "I'm afraid that was
a guess," she admitted. (Lash, Helen and Teacher, *334)*

This interaction demonstrates that Helen took in everything she could about the people around her and enjoyed learning about them. Perhaps even more powerfully, we sense just how much Helen was enjoying the conversation itself and the reporter with whom she was talking. Her overwhelming desire to connect with others, her rapt attentiveness during interactions, and her "rippling laugh" all give away the delight she took in other human beings and the joy she experienced in relating to them.

We have an incredible and almost unlimited ability to observe things about other people. This capacity is innate, but we are free to take it in the direction we choose. What a shame if we use our observational power to discover and dwell on what is wrong with them, criticizing and cataloguing their faults. What a shame when, in truth, we are equally able to adopt an attitude of delighting in others and the many things we are able to notice about them.

People who routinely focus on the flaws of others don't realize that their own enjoyment withers as they do so. Bertrand Russell said, "The secret of happiness is this: let your interests be as wide as possible, and let your reactions to the things and persons that interest you be as far as possible friendly rather than hostile."

Focusing on the single, narrow aspect of physical appearance is another less productive pursuit, even an abuse of our incredible observational skills. In a previous chapter I described my friend who was distracted by the sex appeal of a woman sitting in front of him in a church meeting. In a way, this man's experience demonstrates how powerfully we are drawn to other people, how compelled we are to notice them and think about them. However, he could have taken this pursuit in a much more productive direction. He could have looked at the women and men who surrounded him and appreciated many things about them besides their attractiveness as sex objects. He could have enjoyed the physical beauty that transcends sexuality. He might have thought as he watched them about his past experiences with them as friends and neighbors. He could have noticed in their postures and facial expressions some indications of their personalities and moods. He might have appreciated the vitality of the children, the calm patience of the elderly. He might have watched for signs of affection between family members. He could have observed speakers and singers with an admiring eye and a sympathetic ear.

Although I have lately been trying to deepen my ability to appreciate other people, it is a practice I have always enjoyed. I recall a conversation I had years ago with a girl I was dating. I thought my affection for her had been obvious throughout our friendship, but she said she had been unsure about my feelings for weeks. "At first I thought you liked me," she said, "but then I realized that you treat everyone that way." I still consider that one of the highest compliments I have ever received.

Of course, I am no more able than anyone else to maintain a constant sense of appreciation. However, I have come to accept that when I fail to do so, the problem stems from my own lack of wonder rather than from any real or imagined deficits in the person I am considering. When I am able to maintain my sense of delight, I am constantly amazed at the depth and richness and the many interesting dimensions that can be discovered in people. This makes my clinical work endlessly rewarding: There is always another fascinating story to hear, always more courage to discover, always more qualities to admire.

I have also watched my own potential for appreciating others get derailed time and again as I have succumbed to urges to complain about family members, gossip about acquaintances' perceived flaws and mistakes, and sort through the dirty laundry of politicians and celebrities. Of course, we wouldn't keep returning to these activities if we didn't get some sort of payoff from them. We can feed on the perverse pleasure of faultfinding just as the sex addict does on his fantasies. However, we must remember the price. As with all other manifestations of the intensity trap, immediate indulgence results in a fleeting pleasure even as the long-term costs continue to mount. If this cycle continues, it can result in an utter loss of interest in people's redeeming qualities.

On the other hand, the long-term payoff for observing people in an appreciative way outweighs the effort and discipline this approach demands. Indeed, as our skill in this regard develops, we can uncover rich rewards in even the most seemingly drab circumstances if we simply have another human being to converse with or think about. For Viktor Frankl, the memory of his wife and the company of other inmates—and even some of the guards—provided all the incentive he needed to survive the brutalities of life in a concentration camp. For Torey Haden, a common classroom and a small group of supposedly misfit kids provided enough material to fill volumes and touch the hearts of millions. In *One Child* and her other books she describes the magic that can unfold when we immerse ourselves in someone else's life. Similarly, Stacey Bess described her growing appreciation for the homeless people she met as she taught at the "School with No Name" that sits under a freeway overpass. Haden's books, Frankl's *Man's Search for Meaning*, and Bess's *Nobody Don't Love Nobody* are excellent resources, providing insight and inspiration to those of us who wish to expand our appreciation of others. They provide proof that we need never be bored with our lives as long as other people are in them.

Pick out a family member, co-worker, or neighbor you usually find irritating or uninteresting and study that person as Jane Goodall did her subjects, with curious and loving eyes. Take a step back and put aside your preconceptions. Don't look at this person as someone you know, but discover him or her anew. As you do, make a mental note of the qualities you admire and can take pleasure in. Note the person's appearance—attending, for instance, to the subtle variations in the color and texture of his or her skin. Listen to the person's voice with an appreciative ear. Approach your subject as you would a character in a novel, watching for subtle clues that provide insight into his or her personality and motives. Take the time to enjoy these qualities and the person as a whole. Once you have practiced this exercise with someone you know, you are ready to try it out on complete strangers. As you do, you will discover that Pierre Mac Orlan was right: We truly can find exceptional people everywhere once we have developed a taste for them.

Epilogue: A Final Signpost

Life is not nonstop enjoyment.

Life is no picnic.

It is a struggle.

Too often, however, we view enjoyment as a prize that will come later, a reward for succeeding in the struggle or in one of the myriad little struggles of which *the* struggle is composed. As problems and challenges mount, they erode our hope and leave us doubting that we will ever taste the joy for which we long.

I hope that this book has helped you glimpse an alternative point of view: that we already have everything we need to enjoy ourselves and live full and meaningful lives even in the midst of our struggles.

I hope our exploration has dispelled the notion that enjoyment might be yours at *this* destination or *that* journey's end, and that you're no longer expecting enjoyment around the next turn in the trail or over distant horizons. I hope, instead, that you are spending more time looking down at the trail right beneath you, the dirt just behind you and immediately before you. If your life and energy are more centered in the precious here, in the precious now, and on the precious others you already know or are about to meet, you will have discovered the key to lasting enjoyment.

Sources Cited

"50 Most Beautiful," *People*, 10 May 1999.

Ackerman, Diane, *A Natural History of Love*. New York: Vintage Books, 1994.

———, *A Natural History of the Senses*. New York: Random House, 1990.

"Anita Ekberg Looks Back—and Down," *Parade*, 1 August 1999, 14.

Beach, Johnston, as quoted in *APA Monitor*, January 1999.

Bess, Stacey, *Nobody Don't Love Nobody: Lessons on Love from the School with No Name*. Salt Lake City, UT: Gold Leaf Press, 1994.

Blum, K., J. G. Cull, E. R. Braverman, and D. E. Comings, "Reward Deficiency Syndrome," *American Scientist* 84 (1996): 132–45.

Boteach, Shmuley, *Kosher Sex: A Recipe for Passion and Intimacy*. New York: Doubleday, 1999.

Breathnach, Sarah Ban, *Simple Abundance: A Daybook of Comfort and Joy*. New York: Warner Books, 1995.

Caldwell, Taylor, *A Pillar of Iron*. New York: Doubleday, 1965.

Cline, Victor B., Roger G. Croft, and Steven Courrier, "Desensitization of Children to Television Violence." *Journal of Personality and Social Psychology*, Vol. 27 (1973), no. 3, 360–65.

Cloninger, C., "Neurogenetic Adaptive Mechanisms in Alcoholism." *Science*, 1987, 236, 410–16.

Csikszentmihalyi, Mihaly, *Flow: The Psychology of Optimal Experience*. New York: Harper & Row, 1990.

Douek, E., "Olfaction and Medicine." In *Perfumery: The Psychology and Biology of Fragrance*, ed. S. Van Toller and G. Doll. London: Chapman Hill, 1998.

Ebberfeld, Ingelore, quoted at **http//www.rki.de/GESUND/ARCHIVE/SSMELL.HTM**

Field, Tiffany M., "Massage Therapy Effects." *American Psychologist*, Vol. 53 (1998), no. 12, 1270–81.

Frankl, Viktor E., *Man's Search for Meaning*. New York: Simon and Schuster, 1984.

Freudberg, David, "An Optimist in Spite of All: Helen Keller's Life Story," audiocassette. Cambridge, MA: SounDocumentaries, n.d.

———, "Humankind: A Different Sort of Food," audiocassette. Belmont, MA: Human Media Foundation, n.d., program 11.

Gallup, George, Jr., and F. Newport, "American's Widely Disagree on What Constitutes 'Rich.'" *Gallup Poll Monthly*, July 1990, 28–36.

Gardner, Marilyn, "Advice on Parenting Switches from Laxity to Tighter Discipline," *Christian Science Monitor*, 26 February 1998.

Gaylin, Willard, *Feelings: Our Vital Signs*. New York: Harper & Row, 1979.

Gelb, Michael J., *How to Think Like Leonardo da Vinci: Seven Steps to Genius Every Day*. New York: Delacorte, 1998.

Gilligan, Stephen, "If You Really Knew Me." In *Therapeutic Conversations*, ed. Stephen Gilligan and Reese Price. New York: W. W. Norton, 1993.

Glenn, H. Stephen, and Jane Nelsen, *Raising Self-Reliant Children in a Self-Indulgent World: Seven Building Blocks for Developing Capable Young People*. Rocklin, CA: Prima Publishing & Communications, 1988.

Goldstein, Avram, "Thrills in Response to Music and Other Stimuli." *Physiological Psychology*, Vol. 8 (1980), no. 1, 126–29.

Goleman, Daniel, *Emotional Intelligence*. New York: Bantam, 1995.

Gosman, Fred, *Spoiled Rotten: American Children and How to Change Them*. New York: Warner Books, 1992.

Greenfeld, Karl Taro, "Life on the Edge." *Time*, 6 September 1999, 29–36.

Gutierres, S. E., D. T. Kenrick, and L. Goldberg, "Adverse Effect of Popular Erotica on Judgments on One's Mate." Paper presented at the 91st Annual Convention of the American Psychological Association, Anaheim, CA, 1983.

Haden, Torey L., *One Child*. New York: Avon, 1995.

Harmer, John, *A War We Must Win*. Salt Lake City, UT: Bookcraft, 1999.

Hindustan Times, 11 March 1998.

Junger, Sebastian, "The Lure of Danger." *Men's Journal*, April 1998, 55–58, 131.

Kahneman, Danie, and Jackie Snell, "Predicting a Changing Taste." *Journal of Behavioral Decision Making*, Vol. 5 (1992), 187–200.

Keller, Helen, *Light in My Darkness*, revised and edited by Ray Silverman. Westchester, PA: Chrysalis Books, 1994.

———, "The World through Three Senses," publication unidentified, 220–27.

Kerr, Walter, *Decline of Pleasure*. New York: Simon & Schuster, 1962.

Lash, Joseph P., *Helen and Teacher: The Story of Helen Keller and Anne Sullivan Macy*. New York: Delacorte, 1980.

Lewis, C. S., *The Screwtape Letters*. New York: Simon and Schuster, 1996.

———, *The Weight of Glory and Other Addresses*. Grand Rapids, Mich.: Eerdmans, 1949.

Liebowitz, Michael R., *The Chemistry of Love*. Boston: Little-Brown, 1983.

Lykken, David T., *Happiness: What Studies on Twins Show Us About Nature, Nurture, and the Happiness Set Point*. New York: Golden Books, 1999.

Mallory, George Leigh, 1922, quoted at **http://www.psc.edu/~nystrom/nn_pers.html**

Maxwell, Neal A., *Deposition of a Disciple*. Salt Lake City, UT: Deseret Book, 1976.

———, "Try the Virtue of the Word of God," audiocassette. Provo, UT: Brigham Young University, 1983.

———, *We Will Prove Them Herewith*. Salt Lake City, UT: Deseret Book, 1982.

Miller, Timothy Ray, *How to Want What You Have: Discovering the Magic and Grandeur of Ordinary Existence*. New York: Avon, 1996.

Muller, Wayne, *Sabbath: Restoring the Sacred Rhythm of Rest*. New York: Bantam, 1999.

Myers, David G., *The Pursuit of Happiness: Who Is Happy and Why?* New York: William Morrow, 1992.

Ornstein, Robert, and David Sobel, *Healthy Pleasures*. New York: Perseus Press, 1990.

Parents Television Council, "e-Alerts," at **http://www. parentstv.org**

"Pay Nags at Workers' Job Views," *Chicago Tribune*, 18 October 1987, 10B.

Peck, M. Scott, *The Road Less Traveled*. New York: Simon and Schuster, 1998.

Pert, Candace, *Molecules of Emotion: Why You Feel the Way You Feel*. New York: Scribner, 1997.

"Rich Think Big about Living Well," *Chicago Tribune*, 24 September 1987, 3.

Rossi, Ernest Lawrence, *Twenty-Minute Break: Reduce Stress, Maximize Performance, and Improve Health and Emotional Well-Being Using the New Science of Ultradian Rhythms*. N.p.: Palisades Gateway, 1991.

Sacks, Oliver, *The Man Who Mistook His Wife for a Hat*. New York: Summit Books, 1970.

————, *An Anthropologist on Mars: Seven Paradoxical Tales*. New York: Knopf, 1995.

Schlobin, Roger C., "Children of a Darker God: A Taxonomy of Deep Horror Fiction and Film and Their Mass Popularity," *Journal of the Fantastic in the Arts*, Vol. 1 (1988), no. 1, 25–50.

Scott, Walter, "Personality Profile." *Parade*, 13 June 1999.

Stanley, Thomas J., and William D. Danko, *The Millionaire Next Door: The Surprising Secrets of America's Wealthy*. Atlanta, GA: Longstreet Press, 1996.

Sylvester, Sandra M., "Milton H. Erickson, M.D.: The Wounded

Physician as Healer." In *Ericksonian Methods: The Essence of the Story*, ed. Jeffrey Zeig. New York: Brunner/Mazel, 1994.

"Touch," video episode from *The Mystery of the Senses*, Nova television series.

True Story of the Roman Arena, The, videocassette. Films for the Humanities and Sciences, 1994.

Walton, Gary M., *Beyond Winning: The Timeless Wisdom of Great Philosopher Coaches*. N.p.: Leisure Press, 1992.

Index

Ability, sensory, loss of, 53
Abundance, 6, 27, 104–5
Abuse, drug, 33, 37
Ackerman, Diane, 89–90
Acquisitions and attainments, viii
Addiction, viii; sexual, 11; drug, 19–20; cycle of, 23–25, 29, 33, 68, 73; and tolerance, 26; destructive process of, 29, 95; recovery from, 86; overcoming, 110
Adrenaline, 111
Advertising, 16, 34
Affairs, justification of, 9
Alcohol abuse, 37–38, 86, 90
Anhedonia, 19
Anosmia, 51
Antipornography crusade, 100–102
Appearance, physical, 8–9, 11, 129; and enjoyment, 8–9
Appetite: seductive lies of, 14, 18, 21; advertising and, 17, 21
Appreciation, 6, 14, 103, 130
Attractiveness, sexual, 12
Augustus, 30
Awareness, 114; sense of, 119; sensory, 120; and enjoyment, 124–25

Beach, Johnston, 34
Beauty: satisfaction and, 7–8; stimulation and, 9
Behavior: addictive, viii; antisocial, 38
Bess, Stacey, 131
Biofeedback, 40
Blessings, counting, 107

Blum, Kenneth, 37
Boatman, Michael, 35
Boredom, 26, 37; and divorce, 33
Boteach, Rabbi Shmuley, 82
Brainwaves, 110–11
Brown, Sandra, 111–12
Bryson, Fran, 40
Buddhists, 77, 79
Butt, Ronald, 32

Caesar, Julius, 30
Chamberlain, Jenny, 10–11
Chamberlain, Ryan, 98–99
Chamberlain, Zachary, 10–11
Character, 86
Charity, 77
Childbirth, 10
Children: depriving our, 80–81; boredom and, 89; self-reliant, 104
Chouinard, Yvon, 121
Cicero, 32
Cline, Victor, 41–43
Comfort, 95
Commitment, viii, 25, 86
Completion, yearning for, 89
Compulsion, viii, 37; and drug abuse, 21; and speed, 81–82
Conscience: darkening, 36; heeding the voice of, 92, 102; dulling our, 94
Consequences, drug abuse and, 21
Contentment, 109
Convenience, prioritizing, 82
Courtship, 25
Covey, Stephen, 66–67

Cravings, 27; experiencing, 87, 91
Cruise, Tom, 7, 92
Cynicism, 93

Danger, lure of, 26
Danko, William, 5
Darkness, pornography and, 101–2
Deficiency, reward, 37–38
Degeneracy, 92, 94
Degradation: moral, 31; entertainment and, 34–36; spiritual, 92; warning signs of, 95–96
Delight: sensitivity and, 120, 126; sense of, 130
Deprivation, 73–75; avoidance of, 76–77; Christ and life of, 77–78; practicing, 79; and desire, 84; willingness to undergo, 90
Desensitization, 27, 29, 99; and violence, 32–33; barometer of, 34; conscience and, 93–94, 102
Desire, 28; limiting, 84; experiencing, 87
Discipline, 115
Discomfort, 91; emotional, 87
Dissatisfaction, 9, 26, 89
Divorce, viii; justification of, 9; boredom and, 33
Dopamine, 47
Dreams, reality and, 3
Drug abuse, 33, 37, 71. See also Addiction
Durant, Will, 110

Eating, enjoyment of, 113, 123
Ebberfeld, Ingelore, 53
Ekberg, Anita, 8
Eliot, George, 114
Emotion: bodily response to, 25; experiencing, 39
Empathy, 23–25, 124
Emptiness, 91
Endorphin, 47–48, 70
Enjoyment, vii–ix; escalation and, 15; elusive nature of, 19; lack of, 22; biological, deficit, 37, 43; capacity for, 40, 120; chemicals, 47; full-bodied, 50; experiencing, 61–62; levels of, 64; cycle of, 73; outlook and, 104; of eating, 113; and awareness, 124; of people, 127; struggle and, 133; lasting, 133
Enkephalin, 48, 70
Entertainment: use of violence for, 29–33; degradation and, 34; alternative forms of, 102–3
Enthusiasm, viii
Entitlement, 14, 108
Erickson, Milton, 116–19, 123
Escalation, logic of, 27
Eubank, Mark, 65–66
Evans, Mary Ann (George Eliot), 114

Family, prioritizing, 85
Fantasizing, 11, 82
Fasting, 77, 79–80
Faultfinding, 130–31
Films, 34
Foote, Gordon, 68

Frankl, Viktor, 131
Freedom, priority and, 85
Frog, illustration of the Leopard Green, 94–95
Fulfillment, 74–75

Games: Roman, 32; video, 34
Gandhi, Indira, 109
Gautama, Siddhartha, 77
Gaylin, Willard, 50
Gelb, Michael, 121
Germann, Greg, 35
Gibby, Greg and Darin, 72
Gibson, Mel, 7
Ginseng, 74–75
Girstein, Alisha, 80
Giving, 107
Goals, 13, 79
God: making room for, 76–77; displacing, 77
Goldstein, Avram, 49–50
Goodall, Jane, 127, 131
Gosman, Fred, 80–81
Gratification: immediate, 9, 79, 90–91, 108; delayed, 73–74; and displacing God, 77
Greenfeld, Karl Taro, 33
Growth, despair and, 87

Habits, unhealthy, 11, 95
Habituation, 34
Haden, Torey, 131
Hajj (traveling to Mecca), 77
Haldane, J. B. S., 127
Hamilton, Brutis, 79
Happiness: lasting, 4; and affluence, 5; experiencing, 61; and desire, 82–83
Haraway, Donna, 58
Hare, Robert, 38–39
Harmer, John, 100–102

Health, perception and, 11
Hearts, hardening of, 33
Heroin, 19–20, 33
Home, dream, 3
Hunger, 75; of soul, 91
Hungry ghost, 27
Huntington's Chorea, 62
Hurrying, 108–9

Illusions, optical, 106
Immersion, 104
Impatience, 109
Inadequacy, 89
Incompleteness, feelings of, 87
Inconvenience: maintaining a level of, 81; tolerance for, 108
Indulgence, 79, 131
Infatuation, 9–10
Inspiration, 64–65
Intensification, cycle of, 34
Intensity: trap of, 22–23, 26–28, 108–9, 131; appetite and, 33
Intimacy, 25; abstinence from physical, 82; stress and sexual, 111
Islamic faith, 77

Jesus Christ: on discipleship, 77–78; on sacrifice, 78–79; on suffering, 78
Journal, gratitude, 107
Joy: finding, ix, 133; simple, 97
Junger, Sebastian, 26

Kabbot-Zinn, John, 87
Kahnemen, Danie, 72–73
Keller, Helen, viii, 51, 65; and enjoyment, 75–76, 123–26;

pleasure of, in people,
    127–29
Kennedy, John F., Jr., 7
Kerdchoochuay, Hie, 95
Kerr, Walter, 120–21
Kidman, Nicole, 92
Kinesthetic system, 55

Law, breaking, 89
Leisure, alternative forms
    of, 102–3
Leonardo da Vinci,
    113–14, 121
Lewis, C. S., 87, 90, 97
Life, sanctity of, 95
Light, dimming of
    spiritual, 102
Longing, 104
Lottery winners,
    satisfaction of, 5–6
Love, true, 10
Lykken, David, 121–22

Mallory, George Leigh,
    61–62
Manheim, Camryn, 35
Marriage, viii
Massage, 50, 115
Maxwell, Neal A., 76,
    120
McGary, Steve, 100
Mecca, travel to, 77
Media, influence of, 21,
    33–34
Meditation, 80, 102
Methadone, 20
Methodist church, 92
Miller, Fred, 111–12
Miller, Timothy, 106–7
Millionaires, 6
Miracles, everyday, 126
Moderation, sexual, 82
Mohr, Jay, 35–36
Motivation, power of, 119
Movement: enjoyment of,
    55; avoidance of,
    58–59

Movies, 34
Muhammad, 77, 79
Muller, Wayne, 82–83
Music, response to,
    49–50, 64–65
Myers, David, 104

Nature, human, 14
Necessities, giving up,
    81–82
Neediness, 87
Nielson, Dave and
    Mercie, 84–85

Observance, five pillars
    of, 77
Observation, powers of,
    117
Orlan, Pierre Mac, 132
Overload, emotional, 25
Overstimulation, 9, 26,
    68

Parenting, 81
Parents Television
    Council, 35, 81
Pascal, Blaise, 90
Peace of mind, 109
Peck, M. Scott, 73–74, 90
People, 7
People, enjoyment of
    other, 127
Perception, distorted, 106
Perfection, imagining a
    state of, 90
Perspective, 105–6;
    restoring, 15
Pert, Candace, 47–48,
    122–23
Pfeiffer, Michelle, 7–8
Phenylethylamine (PEA),
    9–10
Photography, awareness
    and, 114–15
Physiology, enjoyment
    and, 47
Pleasure: unsustainable

nature of, viii, 6;
    overload of, system,
    23; of the here and
    now, 63; centers of, in
    brain, 70; and
    deprivation, 75;
    cherishing, 98;
    enjoying simple, 119;
    in our work, 122;
    receptors, 123
Pornography, 9, 82;
    crusade against,
    100–102
Poverty, 78–79
Prayer, 77
Pregnancy, 10
Propaganda, advertising
    and, 16
Proprioceptive system, 55
Prosperity, expectations
    of rising, 5–6
Psychopaths, 38–40
Purification, 102

Rationality, 110
Reactivity, compromised
    physical, 40–41
Real estate, valuation
    and, 3–5
Reality: dreams and, 3;
    appetite and, 18
Receptivity, 115
Receptor: opiate, 47–48;
    pleasure, 48
Recovery, successful, 86
Relaxation, 110
Religion: and sacrifice,
    77; organized, 80
Relinquishment, 77
Repentance, 102
Resentment, 14
Responsiveness: sexual,
    23; blunted emotional,
    40–41
Restoration, 110
Reward deficiency
    syndrome, 37, 40

Rewards: immediate, 23; sacrifice and, 79
Rich, Steve, 72
Rodgers, Ken, 60–61
Roman Empire, 29–33
Russell, Bertrand, 129

Sabbath, observing, 82–83
Sacks, Oliver, 52
Sacrifice, Jesus Christ and, 78
Salat (five compulsory daily prayers), 77
Satisfaction, viii, 73; and beauty, 7–8; as elusive goal, 14, 18, 22–23
Scarcity, abundance and, 27
Scents, 48, 135
Schlobin, Roger C., 34
Scott, Walter, 92
Scripture, study of, 102
Self-control, 56, 110
Self-destruction, 110
Self-discipline, 79–80
Self-pity, 13, 104
Self-stimulation, 38
Self-transformation, 89
Seneca, 31
Sense(s), 48–54; sixth, 55
Sensitivity, 68, 73, 93; endangering, 95; restoring, 97; spiritual, 101; increasing, 115; delight and, 120; and empathy, 124
Serenity, 80
Sex, television and, 33
Sexuality, 11; moderation and, 82; movies and, 99–100

Shalit, Wendy, 27
Sharing, 107
Siegel, Bernie, 111
Silence, 80
Siyam (fasting), 77
Snell, Jackie, 72–73
Spirituality, return to, 77, 91, 93
Standards: decline of, in television, 35; lowering of, 36
Stanley, Thomas, 5
St. Augustine, 30–31
Stimulation: increasing, viii, 22, 26; desensitization to, 25; self-, 38; chemicals and, 47; auditory, 49; tactile, 50; sensory, 49–54; artificially intense, 69; foregoing, 79
Stress, 110–11
Struggle, enjoyment and, 133
Suffering: inevitability of, 77; Jesus Christ and, 78–79; rewards of, 97
Sullivan, Annie, 75–76
Surgery, cosmetic, 8

Taste, 49
Television: daytime, 33–34; degradation and, 36; desensitizing effects of, 41–43; freedom from, 81
Temptation: drugs and, 20–21; experiencing, 87
Therapy, massage, 115
Thrill-seeking, 25

Titus, 30
Tolerance: addiction and, 26; of violence, 31
Tradition, family, 56–58
Tranquillity, Sabbath, 82
Trap, intensity, 22–23, 26–28, 100

Underarousal, 39–40
Underresponsiveness, 37
Understimulation, 37

Vandalism, 89
Video games, 34
Violence: use of, for entertainment, 29–33; and desensitization, 32; television and, 33–34, 41–43; movies and, 99–100
Vulgarity, 95

Want, handling, 85, 87
Wealth, enjoyment of, 5, 104
Weather, 66
Weiler, Judith, 80
Wesley, John, 92–93, 96
Wonder, cultivating, 127
Work, taking pleasure in, 122
Worship, fasting as act of, 79–80
Wright, Doug, 93–94

Yom Kippur, 80

Zakat (charity), 77
Zukav, Gary, 87